Supernatural

McDougal & Associates
Servants of Christ and stewards of the mysteries of God

Supernatural

Living Under an Open Heaven

by

Eddie T. Rogers

Original cover design by Lara York
zoecreationgrafx@bellsouth.net

Published by:

McDougal & Associates
P.O. Box 194
Greenwell Springs, LA 70739-0194
www.thepublishedword.com

McDougal & Associates is dedicated to the spreading of the Gospel of Jesus Christ to as many people as possible in the shortest time possible.

ISBN 13: 978-0-9777053-2-0
ISBN 10: 0-9777053-2-3
Printed in the United States of America
For Worldwide Distribution

DEDICATION

I dedicate this work to my future inheritance through my children and grandchildren, as well as the next generation of supernatural believers who will take this move of God to the next level of revival—the revival that never ends.

To my daughter and son-in-law, Shelley and Dana Thompson. To my grandkids (to date), Collin and Brandon Thompson. To my son Jesse Rogers. And to the host of youth who will take my generation's "ceiling" and allow it to become their "floor."

ACKNOWLEDGMENTS

It is impossible to go from manuscript to completed book without the help of many individuals. I wish to acknowledge some of those without whom this project could not have been accomplished.

Thank you, LARA YORK, for your tireless work and dedication on the cover design to "make me happy." And I *am* happy!

Thank you, RALENA BURGESS, for your gifting, dedication and skill to see through the "context" to find my grammatical errors.

Thanks to my best friend in life, MICHELLE (my wife), for your constant encouragement, prayers and belief in me.

Finally, I have to thank my dear friend and longtime relationship, CHARLES CARRIN, for introducing the Holy Spirit to some of our old friends a long time ago. In 1994 we had made a church plant while inheriting a "row" of former members from my father's church after his passing the year before. The "row," as we called it, consisted of a group of older members who became a part of the church because of their relationship with him.

Unfortunately, the "row" never moved or came forward for ministry when the Holy Spirit came to visit our newly-formed congregation. They were staunch observers, but never participators ... that is until Brother Charles came to minister.

The first night he marched down the center aisle to the "row," where he promptly commanded them to exit their seats and enter the aisle. As they stepped into the aisle, Charles laid hands on them and every single one of them ended up doing some quality carpet time. "Hello, Holy Spirit!"

It was something I will never forget, nor will I ever forget the love, warmth and caring you have shown to us, as well as to every other ministry son and daughter you've touched. Thank you, Charles.

Then Jacob awoke from his sleep and said, "Surely the Lord *is in this place, and I did not know it."*

And he was afraid and said, "How awesome is this place! This is none other than the house of God, and this is THE GATE OF HEAVEN."

Genesis 28:16-17, Emphasis added

Editor's Note

Speaking of "an open heaven" presents us with a rather unique grammatical problem. As those who believe that Heaven is a very real place, just as real as New York or London, we always capitalize that name. The term "an open heaven," however, refers to the atmosphere over us. "An open heaven" refers to an unhindered access to the real Heaven. Therefore the reader will note that we sometimes capitalize the word Heaven and sometimes we don't. This is the reason. "An open heaven" is a gateway to the real Heaven, or, as Jacob put it, *"THE GATE OF HEAVEN."*

CONTENTS

FOREWORD

A few weeks after I was saved in 1948 I remember standing in our yard in Miami, Florida, and telling my brother, "There is something *more!*" In spite of my having had a spectacular salvation experience, in my heart I knew there had to be another God-empowering encounter awaiting me. I said it again, "There *is* something more!"

My disappointment was overwhelming when he answered, "No, Charles, there is nothing more. When you were saved you got it all." For a moment I only stared at him. As he walked away, I remember thinking, "He may not need something more, but *I* do!"

That was a long time ago. In another year I begin my sixtieth year of Christian ministry, and today I will gladly tell you, not only is there "something more," but I have found it! Eddie Rogers' book, *Supernatural,* will help you get there too. Its truths are what I desperately wanted sixty years ago.

During the intervening years, I've had hundreds and hundreds of books come across my desk. Some were big with little messages, and others were little with big messages. A few were like cannons with rifle-sized powder, and there were those rare rifle-sized books that could blow bigger holes in the enemy's camp than other cannons could hope to accomplish. How I wish my early years of ministry could have had the benefit of Eddie Rogers' rifle! Like a well-aimed gun, this compact book targets the Holy Spirit's manifestations from the biggest to the smallest. Eddie will lead you from "Finding the Divine Order" and "Overcoming Doctrinal Limitations" to discovering "Whose Kingdom Are We Building?" Read it and be blessed!

Charles Carrin
Author, Evangelist
Member of the Word, Spirit, Power Conference Team
With R.T. Kendall and Jack Taylor

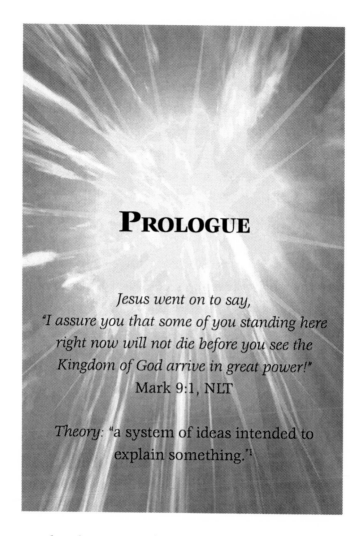

PROLOGUE

Jesus went on to say,
"I assure you that some of you standing here
right now will not die before you see the
Kingdom of God arrive in great power!"
Mark 9:1, NLT

Theory: "a system of ideas intended to
explain something."[1]

It has been my observation that most Christians live in theory. Either they live with the God who *did* in the past or the One who *will do* in the future. To them, the God of the present exists, but only in theory. Our theology is seemingly defined by the miracles we no longer need or the miracles we will one day see "in the millennium." The problem with both these ideologies is that they don't require any faith for the present.

The Bible becomes a historical book in context of great things that *were* and a prophetic book of great things that *will be,* but again, no faith is required. If you can explain an idea that doesn't involve your faith pressing in for something now, you no longer have a supernatural involvement in earth's affairs. Church becomes a comfort zone of all things religious and absolutely nothing supernaturally spiritual.

Somehow the possibility of a *now* God doing "stuff" *right now* (as in the present) becomes a threat to our comfort and jeopardizes our predetermined safety net of denominational doctrine. Rules of religion keep me *safe* from things I don't understand. Unfortunately, religion can't keep me safe; only Jesus can.

PLAYING IT SAFE

In 1994, while on a quest to find the living God of the *now,* I attended a revival meeting of a South African evangelist. A pastor friend advised me that I would find what (or Whom) I was looking for there. The service was typical of any Charismatic service I had attended before. The loud music and dancing didn't bother me—even though I had been raised in a traditional Baptist church. Everything was "safe" (*safe,* defined as "under control") ... until the evangelist entered the sanctuary. Then all Heaven broke loose.

From the back of the church I heard a commotion and turned to see what was going on. I saw a woman, probably in her early fifties, saying "something" with a loud voice.

But the sound that was coming out of her was neither female nor human. I thought, *"Hmm, I've never seen that in church before."* A few minutes later she was free, smiling and crying for joy.

Do You Want that in a "To-Go" Box?

For most Christians that would be God "out of the box." In actual fact, that is God within the box, that is, within the definitions of the described workings of the anointing and ministry. Jesus said:

> **And as you go, preach, saying, "The kingdom of heaven is at hand." Heal the sick, cleanse the lepers, raise the dead, cast out demons. Freely you have received, freely give.** Matthew 10:7-8

The Kingdom work is often a confrontational work, so if you don't like confrontation, then doing the work of the Kingdom isn't for you. Certainly that does not imply that we are to be rude, callous or unsympathetic. It does, however, mean that when confronted with the kingdom of darkness, we take no prisoners. I am to usurp authority over sickness, disease and demons alike and bring the situation I am facing into the *now* of *"as it is in Heaven!"*

Jesus declared that one validation of the Kingdom being present was victory over demonic conflict:

> **But if I cast out demons by the Spirit of God [the**

*anointing], surely the kingdom of God has come
upon you.*   Matthew 12:28

Possession Is "All of the Law"

To do the work of the Kingdom, I can no longer live in
theory, nor can I imitate what I do not actually possess.
Many, it seems, can wear expensive suits and drive expensive cars and all the while they are held captive by debt
and discouragement. That is merely imitating the blessing
without possessing it!

When Peter took the lame man by the hand in Acts
chapter 3, he didn't say, "For such as I think I have" or,
"For such as it appears I have." No, for Peter, *theory* wasn't
involved. The reality of having been with Jesus produced
the results of the Kingdom:

*Then Peter said, "Silver and gold I do not have,
but what I do have I give you: In the name of
Jesus Christ of Nazareth, rise up and walk."*
                                             Acts 3:6

"But WHAT I DO HAVE I give you." What do I have to
give? A theory? A hope? A promise? Or do I possess the
authority and power to bring an invasion of Kingdom realities? If I do not possess the ability to bring revival and
open the heavens wherever I am, then the question is: Am
I willing to *do* whatever it takes or *go* wherever the pres-

ence and power of God is falling and let Him change me so that I can then bring change to others?

Theory is fine for science projects, but when it comes to the Kingdom, there isn't any room for guess work. Jesus told Pilate His Kingdom was not of this world (see John 18:36). If His Kingdom isn't of *this* world, the natural realm we live in, then it must be other-worldly. His throne is the world of the *Supernatural.* And, like Enoch, it's time for us to step on over to the other side.

End Notes:
1. Definition from *The Compact Oxford English Dictionary*

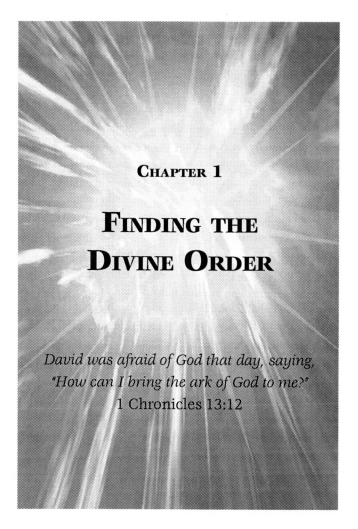

CHAPTER 1

FINDING THE
DIVINE ORDER

David was afraid of God that day, saying,
"How can I bring the ark of God to me?"
1 Chronicles 13:12

N estled comfortably between an elderly grand-
father and his grandson, I sat peering over
the front seat of the car. Our driver, dressed
in clean blue overalls and a brown felt fedora hat, sat
relaxed, with one arm resting out the open window. His
wife calmly sat in the passenger seat, smiling and hum-
ming a song, as she reflected on the service that had just
ended. Her hair was long, but neatly folded into a bun

underneath her black Sunday-go-to-meeting hat. Her dress was plain and simple, delicately arrayed in a flower pattern.

As we drove down an isolated country road, the landscape surrounding us consisted of rolling wooded hills in a very rural environment. From my perspective, it appeared that I had traveled back in time fifty or sixty years. Everyone seemed to be quite content with our car, our drive and our setting. I turned and glanced over my shoulder to look at the road behind us, and that's when I realized that something wasn't quite right.

Mounted where the trunk of our car should have been was a white frame church. That's right, our car was attached to a church—steeple and all. Wherever we drove, we carried this church with us. Actually, apart from the church "thingy," it was a delightfully scenic ride. Suddenly, I woke up. (Wow! Shades of Steve Martin's *The Jerk!*)

As I lay in bed, I thought to myself, *"Well, it doesn't take a great leap of faith to believe You're trying to tell me something, Lord. So speak. Your servant is listening."*

Then, very clearly, the still, small voice of the Holy Spirit began to reveal to my spirit the interpretation. He began to show me how many leaders assume they are still in control, "driving the church" where they want it to go. They don't realize they cannot "drive the church" where they want it to go. God alone is in the driver's seat, and He will take the church where He wants it to go.

The dated clothes and surroundings weren't so much

to reveal a bygone era, but rather the comfort zones of church politics. They revealed a don't-change-a-thing mentality. Regardless of denomination or religious affiliation, the supernatural church will be a church in divine order. Only when divine order becomes the church order will the presence of God become manifest in the midst of the church.

LOVELY ARE YOUR DWELLING PLACES

Nothing in all of the Old Testament represents an open heaven more than the Ark of the Covenant. It was the manifest dwelling place of God on earth. From above the Mercy Seat, God spoke with Moses:

> *And there I will meet with you, and I will speak with you from above the mercy seat, from between the two cherubim which are on the ark of the Testimony.* Exodus 25:22

It is interesting to note that even Israel's enemies associated God's presence with the Ark of the Covenant:

> *So the people sent to Shiloh, that they might bring from there the ark of the covenant of the LORD of hosts, WHO DWELLS BETWEEN THE CHERUBIM. ... And when the ark of the covenant of the LORD came into the camp, all Israel shouted so loudly that the earth shook. Now when the Phil-*

21

*istines heard the noise of the shout, they said,
"What does the sound of this great shout in the
camp of the Hebrews mean?" Then they under-
stood that the ark of the LORD had come into the
camp. SO THE PHILISTINES WERE AFRAID,
FOR THEY SAID, "GOD HAS COME INTO THE
CAMP!"*   1 Samuel 4:4-7, Emphasis added

DAVID'S DESIRE

If nothing in the Old Testament represents an open
heaven more than the Ark of God, then no one individual
more represents a desire for God's presence than King
David. His hunger was unparalleled, and his longing for
the manifest presence of God is witnessed in his writings
and subsequent actions:

*A Psalm of David when he was in the wilderness
of Judah.*

*O God, You are my God;
Early will I seek You;
My soul thirsts for You;
My flesh longs for You
In a dry and thirsty land
Where there is no water."*   Psalm 63:1

David's deep desire was to bring the presence of God,
the Ark of the Covenant, to Jerusalem. It was more than

a casual longing or a fleeting momentary wish. This wasn't window-shopping and thinking, "My, I would like adding that garment to my wardrobe." This was a burning passion that craved God's presence above everything else. A desire that was rightly motivated by God Himself drove David to do the *right* thing the *wrong* way.

When God has revealed a divine order of business, then our excuses for not following that order will often end in judgment. If not judgment, at least a marked absence of the presence of God. Today it would mean an absence of miracles, signs and wonders, as well as salvations. Simply put, *"having a form of godliness but denying its power"* (2 Timothy 3:5). Regretfully, the most disheartening factor involves those who have been deceived into believing they are still in the driver's seat, and the church is "okay."

An authentic desire for the supernatural realms of God will cause us to abandon anything that would prevent God from showing up in our services and everything that would prevent us from finding Him. I'm not referring to following legalistic codes of religion but of having an unadulterated viewpoint of not grieving the Holy Spirit anywhere at anytime.

DAVID'S FRUSTRATION

David's desire to bring the presence of God home was right, but his method was wrong, simply because God had previously revealed the correct procedure for carry-

SUPERNATURAL

ing the Ark. The divine order had been made known. David's *desire* became his *frustration.* Frustration is the feeling that accompanies the experience of being thwarted in attaining your goals.

David's first attempt to accomplish his goal in bringing the Ark home failed because he followed the example of the Philistines, by placing the Ark on an ox cart and not following the divine order. It was a serious failure:

> *And when they came to Nachon's threshing floor, Uzzah put out his hand to the ark of God and took hold of it, for the oxen stumbled. Then the anger of the LORD was aroused against Uzzah, and God struck him there for his error; and he died there by the ark of God ... . So David would not move the ark of the LORD with him into the City of David; but David took it aside into the house of Obed-Edom the Gittite.*
>
> 2 Samuel 6:6-7 and 10

Perhaps your desire to see the supernatural release of an open heaven in your church, your city or your ministry has reached the point of frustration. Frustration is a bad thing, only when we stop pursuing our desire for God's manifest presence. Frustration is a good thing when it causes us to inwardly examine ourselves as to why our right desire has been delayed. Remember, delay isn't denial.

TIMING IS EVERYTHING

We must also remember that a desire delayed does not mean we are out of divine order. There may be certain events for which the time is just not yet right:[1]

You will arise and have mercy on Zion;
For the time to favor her,
Yes, the set time, has come.   Psalm 102:13

But when the time has come and still it does not manifest, then it's time to check the divine order. For example 1 Corinthians 12:28 tells us that God has appointed, or set, in the Church first apostles, then prophets, third teachers, and after that other manifestations of gifts. To further accentuate this point, Ephesians 2:20 acknowledges apostles and prophets working together to establish the foundation of the household of God. Where were apostles and prophets set? In the Church.

The absence of divine order is to *not* recognize those ministry gifts as being valid today. This was a struggle for me personally, since the church I was raised in didn't acknowledge these gifts. If God "set" these in the Church, then only God has a right to remove them—not committee's, denominations or theologians. And He did set them there:

And He Himself gave some to be apostles, some
prophets, some evangelists, and some pastors and

> *teachers, for the equipping of the saints for the work of ministry, for the edifying of the body of Christ, till we all come to the unity of the faith and of the knowledge of the Son of God, to a perfect man, to the measure of the stature of the fullness of Christ.* Ephesians 4:11-13

What the Bible says alone should suffice to prove that apostles and prophets are valid today, but more importantly the roles these gifts play in the divine order are essential for an open heaven. Even if your denomination doesn't recognize or acknowledge such in their "religious order," it needn't keep you from personally yielding to God's order. I would rather lay church politics aside and run the risk of losing colleagues, positions and reputation than miss positioning myself under an open heaven and experiencing a visitation of God.

DAVID'S DESPERATION

When God has revealed the known order, we are without excuse if we fail to follow it. Because David's desire for God's presence was greater than his frustration, it allowed his *frustration* to become *desperation.*

David's desperation for the presence of God and an open heaven caused him to ask the question, *"How can I bring the ark of God to me?"* (1 Chronicles 13:12). In other words, "It doesn't matter what it costs! Just find a way to bring me into the presence of God!"

Desperation is the embodiment of extreme urgency because of great need or desire. Desperation will produce actions of a "last resort" nature. Contentment and desperation are at opposite ends of the rate-my-spiritual-condition chart. However, it is while in the "frustration" mode that we determine which direction we will go.

Frustration will either cause you to give up your desire and become content with the status quo of church politics (the religious order) or drive you to desperation to find the divine order. Whatever the order may be for you as an individual, as a church or as a ministry, desperation will cause you to pay the price for an open heaven.

An Open Heaven Releases God's Favor

An open heaven is a place where the blessings of God flow. It is a place where strivings cease and the profuse favor of God abounds. It is a place where the "suddenlies of success" flourish. When the house of Obed-Edom received the Ark of the Lord for three months, the Lord blessed Obed-Edom and his entire household. When you live under an open heaven, even those associated with you will be blessed:

> *Now it was told King David, saying, "The LORD has blessed the house of Obed-Edom and all that belongs to him, because of the ark of God." So David went and brought up the ark of God from*

the house of Obed-Edom to the City of David with
gladness.   2 Samuel 6:12

David found the divine order and brought the Ark up by having the Levites carry its poles on their shoulders, as commanded by Moses.[2] With much sacrifice, extreme praise and worship and ecstatic joy, the Ark was successfully brought to the City of David. The heavens were open, and the supernatural, tangible presence of God was experienced.

I am convinced that two keys to opening the heavens are sacrifice and extreme praise and worship. Joy will always follow those two ingredients, when the presence of God is our sole delight and nothing more:

You will show me the path of life;
IN YOUR PRESENCE IS FULLNESS OF JOY;
At Your right hand are pleasures forevermore.
                              Psalm 16:11, Emphasis added

AN OPEN HEAVEN WILL BRING OPPOSITION

Regrettably, an open heaven will give opportunity for jealousy to manifest from those who are content with the way things are. Saul's daughter (and David's wife) Michal represented the old order of things. Like Michal, those of the former order who are left to criticize the new things of God do so at their own peril. Those who fail to embrace the divine order will be left barren in the Kingdom of

God. Such will always be the case with those of a prior order who will not accept the changes that occur when "revival" under an open heaven comes to town.

It is God's desire to include those of the preceding order and bring them into the new. However, for those reluctant to participate, He will do it without them. For many, it will be the fear of losing the prominence and popularity they enjoyed in the previous order. It is easier to become judgmental and critical, rather than embrace the fact that a new generation just might carry the glory to a greater degree than the former.

Like the church in the dream, many can and will continue to do "church business" without the manifest presence of God. They will continue to enjoy their Sunday ride with "the church" and feel good about doing it. In the meantime, a portal is forming over a raggedy-looking tent of meeting. Desire that should have ended with frustration has turned into fervent desperation. Radical worship is ascending into the heavenlies, and passionate worshippers are crying out to God for more.

Get ready, for all Heaven is about to break loose.

End Notes:
1. I believe it is always God's time. Our time may not have come due to our lack of spiritual maturity, obedience, motives, etc.
2. See 1 Chronicles 15.

29

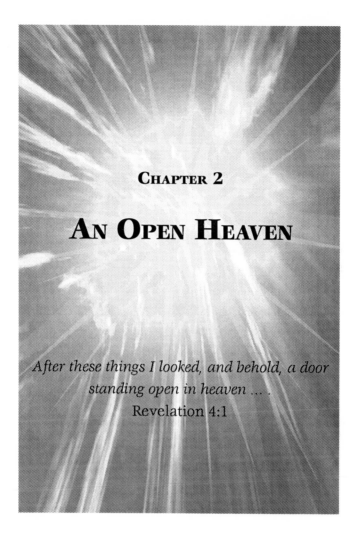

CHAPTER 2

AN OPEN HEAVEN

*After these things I looked, and behold, a door
standing open in heaven ....*
Revelation 4:1

There are several references in scripture that point to an open heaven. One of them is found in Genesis 28, where the Bible records Jacob's dream of a ladder being set up from earth to Heaven and the angels ascending and descending upon it. The key point of an open heaven is this: *"Surely the LORD is in this place"* (Genesis 28:16). An open heaven is recognized because God is there. His works, His love and His presence are being manifest in a tangible way.

The supernatural of God is released under an open heaven. The heavenly invades the earthly and subjugates the natural to the pattern of Heaven. Under an open heaven miracles are easy. Healing, deliverance, signs and wonders and provision, under Heaven's terms, are effortlessly met. Heaven isn't limited, so an open heaven eliminates the word *impossible.*

An open heaven may be in one geographical location and not another. Jacob recognized the Lord was in *that* place, as opposed to not being recognized in another. The concept of an open heaven is not a contradiction to the truth of God's omnipresence. He is everywhere at once, but an open heaven is a demonstration of His manifest presence invading a person, a church, a city or a region.

AN OPEN-HEAVEN EXPERIENCE

In July 1995, while at a summer campmeeting in St. Louis, Missouri, the heavens opened in the place we were meeting, and I witnessed, through my natural eyes, the glory of the Lord sweep into the auditorium. A huge cloud billowed into the arena, rolling and tumbling across the floor and then onto the platform where the speaker was standing. I had no way of knowing if others were seeing what I was seeing or not.

As the cloud encompassed the people on the lower levels, they began to jump out of their seats and run around the platform that was set up on the floor of the arena. Heaven had come to meet earth, and the result was a holy pandemonium. I left the building extremely intoxicated on the heavenly visitation. That following Sunday the same anointing was released in the church where I was then pastor. We had carried the impartation of it back to the place of our service.

Another biblical example of a region with an open heaven is found in Saul's attempt to capture David. In an almost humorous story, Saul sends three groups of messengers to take David captive.[1] As they approach the city, a group of prophets are prophesying, with Samuel standing as leader over them, and the messengers come under an "open heaven" and begin to prophesy themselves. Frustrated, Saul makes the journey to do the work himself, ending up on the ground, prophesying all day and all night.

What had happened? He came into the place where God had opened the heavens, and a manifestation of His presence took place.

Modern-Day Examples

The Azusa Street outpouring in Los Angeles a century ago brought people from around the world to capture a "taste of Heaven" and take it back to their places of residence and impart it there. During the "Toronto Blessing," people came from all over the world to experience the open heaven that had manifested in that city. Other ex-

33

amples would be the Lakeland Revival at Carpenter's Home Church, as well as the Pensacola Revival, that took place in the state of Florida in the 1990s.

Not only can an open heaven reside over a geographical location, but I also believe certain individuals can carry a special authority from God to open the heavens in localities that have been previously closed. These individuals, like Charles Finney, are in a special office and possess a special ability and influence granted by Heaven, a special *exsousia* {ex-oo-see'-ah}. This Greek word can be defined as: "The power of rule or government; the power of Him whose will and commands must be submitted to by others and obeyed."[2]

In Charles Finney's autobiography, he speaks of people crossing the county line where he was conducting revival meetings, and they would immediately fall under conviction, weeping for repentance. They had crossed the border into the "Throne Zone!" Another time it was recorded that as he took a tour of a factory, workers "fell out under the power of God." He carried with him an "open heaven" wherever he went.

Men told Smith Wigglesworth, while traveling in a train car, that his mere presence brought them under conviction. He, in turn, led them in a prayer of repentance for salvation. He was another example of a man carrying about a mantle for an "open heaven."

I believe there are many individuals living today who carry the identical anointing. At the same time, I believe many are being raised up in this hour who will embrace this anointing, until the kingdoms of the earth become the kingdoms of our God.

I know of ministers who have gone into regions where the heavens were seemingly brass and others had experienced only minimal results. Yet, when these anointed ones go to these very same regions with Heaven's authority and power, the profuse favor of God comes upon them, and they are granted audiences with kings, presidents, prime ministers and other heads of state. The region becomes an open heaven because they are carrying Heaven's mantle.

For Every Positive ...

Of course, there is usually a negative for every positive, and with an open heaven, there is no exception. The negative in this case most often comes from those who do not understand the principle. Their personal inexperience is the basis for how they interpret and view the principles of scripture and their relevance for them today, biblical examples or not. Nor do they accept the personal experiences of others, experiences that validate a scriptural principle. They are caught up in the "Thomas syndrome." Nothing personal against Thomas, because my middle name is Thomas, but like him, these people say, "I won't believe it until I see it." To which we must reply, as Jesus did, *"O ye of little faith."*

Throughout the years I have heard two statements repeated over and over again:

- "I don't see why you have to go to a meeting in some other town to meet God."
- "God is sovereign, and if He wants to visit us, He will."

In both of these cases, without exception, those who voice these comments are *not* living under an open heaven. They are very negative and complain about those who pursue God in this way. This is sad, but true.

PLEASE STAND HERE

Throughout the Scriptures, God would often speak to those He wanted to use to go to a specific place, and in that place, He would meet them. For instance:

Now the LORD had said to Abram: "Get out of your country, from your family and from your father's house, TO A LAND THAT I WILL SHOW YOU."
Genesis 12:1, Emphasis added

Then He said, "Take now your son, your only son Isaac, whom you love, and GO TO THE LAND OF MORIAH, and offer him there as a burnt offering ON ONE OF THE MOUNTAINS OF WHICH I SHALL TELL YOU." Genesis 22:2, Emphasis added

Then the LORD said to Moses, "Come up to Me ON THE MOUNTAIN and be there; and I will give you

tablets of stone, and the law and commandments
which I have written, that you may teach them."
SO MOSES AROSE WITH HIS ASSISTANT JOSHUA,
AND MOSES WENT UP TO THE MOUNTAIN OF
GOD.   Exodus 24:12-13, Emphasis added

God also designated specific cities as a place of refuge.
These selected cities were places of safety and protection
for individuals who had committed accidental crimes:

You shall appoint three cities on this side of the
Jordan, and three cities you shall appoint in the
land of Canaan, which will be cities of refuge.
                Numbers 35:14

If the people who had taken refuge in these cities
chose to leave the confines of the city limits, then their
life was in their own hands.

DISCERNING WHAT THE SPIRIT IS SAYING

Rather than belabor the point endlessly, let's summa-
rize and conclude. A frequent word I keep hearing from
the prophets is the word "portal." When God wants to em-
phasize something to the Body of Christ, you will begin to
hear a consistent recurring word, or theme, from many
ministry voices to make clear to us that this is a *rhema*
word by the Spirit. In computer "lingo," a *portal* is "a site
that the owner positions as an entrance to other sites on

the Internet." In the noun form, *portal* can mean "a grand and imposing entrance (often extended metaphorically.)"[3]

To put this in perspective, God, the Owner of an open heaven, desires to place a "portal" of His presence over our gathering places, our homes and even our individual lives. An indication of this is revealed in Isaiah:

> *Then the LORD will create above every dwelling place of Mount Zion, and above her assemblies, a cloud and smoke by day and the shining of a flaming fire by night. For over all the glory there will be a covering. And there will be a tabernacle for shade in the daytime from the heat, for a place of refuge, and for a shelter from storm and rain.*
> Isaiah 4:5-6

Our God wants us to have access to all of the other "sites" that come with an open heaven—salvation, healing, health and provision:

> *And the LORD will grant you plenty of goods, in the fruit of your body, in the increase of your livestock, and in the produce of your ground, IN THE LAND of which the LORD swore to your fathers to give you. THE LORD WILL OPEN TO YOU HIS GOOD TREASURE, THE HEAVENS, to give the rain to your land in its season, and to bless all the work of your hand. You shall lend to many nations, but you shall not borrow. And the*

Lord will make you the head and not the tail; you shall be above only, and not be beneath, if you heed the commandments of the Lord your God, which I command you today, and are careful to observe them.

Deuteronomy 28:11-13, Emphasis added

The Example of the Wise Men

The book of Luke records the journey of eastern astronomers who had observed an unusual "star" in the heavens and, therefore, followed it until they found the young child, Jesus. Whether or not they had received an angelic visitation and invitation, as did the shepherds, is unknown. However, both shepherds and wise men had to travel to where Jesus was.

The Greek language offers two different descriptive words for Jesus at the time of their respected visits. For the shepherds, it offers the word, *brephos* {bref'-os}, describing "a babe or infant":

And they came with haste and found Mary and Joseph, and THE BABE lying in a manger.

Luke 2:16, Emphasis added

For those whom we have come to call "wise men," it offers the word *paidion* {pahee-dee'-on} which usually describes "a young child, a little boy or girl":

SUPERNATURAL

And when they had come into the house, they saw THE YOUNG CHILD with Mary His mother, and fell down and worshiped Him.

Matthew 2:11, Emphasis added

Note that He was no longer in a manger. In fact, many scholars believe that Jesus was already about two years old at the time of the arrival of the wise men, and they cite the fact that Herod had all the male children two years of age and under put to death (see Matthew 2:16). In light of that, it was a long and expensive journey which these men had to undertake to meet the King of Kings. It cost them a great deal personally to go to the place of an open heaven, not to mention the expensive gifts they brought to Him. However, what they received in return was priceless.

THY KINGDOM COME, THY WILL BE DONE ...

At this very moment, I believe the portals of Heaven are forming around us. In certain geographical locations, as well as with certain individual ministries, we are about to experience an outpouring of heavenly manifestations. A visitation of Kingdom proportions is coming on a new generation of God chasers who will begin where all others have left off. The question is, "Will you be a candidate to pursue this supernatural holy convocation, or will you be content to wait and see?"

And He said to him, "Most assuredly, I say to you, hereafter you shall see heaven open, and the angels of God ascending and descending upon the Son of Man."
John 1:51

End Notes:
1. See 1 Samuel 19:20-24
2. Meaning from www.blueletterbible.org
3. Definition from www.onelook.com

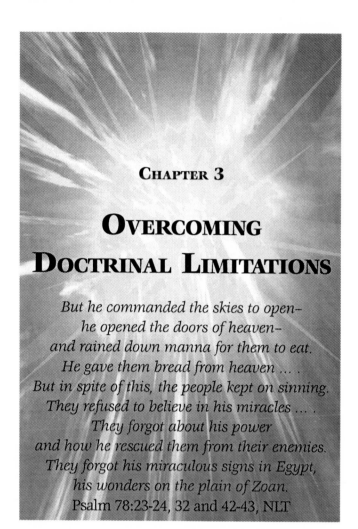

CHAPTER 3

OVERCOMING
DOCTRINAL LIMITATIONS

But he commanded the skies to open—
he opened the doors of heaven—
and rained down manna for them to eat.
He gave them bread from heaven ... .
But in spite of this, the people kept on sinning.
They refused to believe in his miracles ... .
They forgot about his power
and how he rescued them from their enemies.
They forgot his miraculous signs in Egypt,
his wonders on the plain of Zoan.
Psalm 78:23-24, 32 and 42-43, NLT

Again and again they ... limited the Holy One of
Israel.   Psalm 78:41

L iving in the supernatural is "potentially" a reality for every believer. However, as Psalm 78
points out, we are not unlike Israel, disbelieving God's signs, wonders and provision. The Western church
has built ideologies and doctrines that support their disbe-

lief in the supernatural, a doctrinal theology that excuses signs and wonders, the baptism of the Holy Spirit, the gifts of the Spirit, angelic visitations and manifestations of Heaven on earth. These are all supported by the Bible, and doctrines that deny them are called *"doctrines of demons"*:

> *Now the Spirit expressly says that in latter times some will depart from the faith, giving heed to deceiving spirits and doctrines of demons.*
>
> 1 Timothy 4:1

Granted, that seems to be a harsh and cruel statement, and I must point out that I'm not criticizing my brothers and sisters in the Lord who choose to adhere to such doctrines. At the same time, I have to point out that these are the doctrines that hinder the church from pressing into the principles of Kingdom living.

Cessationist theology[1] has done more damage to the church than one can imagine. It sets boundaries on a boundless God. It puts limitations on a limitless Savior. It places borders around a borderless Kingdom. It displaces faith with facts. It places prominence on the pulpit and leaves powerlessness in the pews. It forces reins onto the Holy Spirit and removes the supernatural empowerment from the Church as a whole. It relishes in building walls within a Church that was built without walls.

BELIEVE IT ... OR NOT!

Ironically, most of the church which embraces

cessationist theology usually adheres to a strict and literal interpretation of the Scriptures, in effect, giving a seemingly logical excuse for why "God doesn't do that anymore." The very thing Cessationists apologetically defend, the inerrancy of scripture, is then turned around and used to deny that things such as miracles, healings, speaking in tongues, apostles, prophets, etc. are applicable today. This, to my way of thinking, presents a total contradiction.

Heresy hunters[2] seem bent on destroying anything they cannot rationally explain or understand, and so they denounce it as being not of God, a reaction of the flesh or even demonic. In this way, they totally disregard the scriptural fact: *"But our God is in heaven; He does whatever He pleases"* (Psalm 115:3).

We are told by anti-supernatural voices to place no value on personal experiences. They would much rather hold to a formal and safe box of scriptures that is left nice and tidy on the pews each Sunday versus someone outside the clergy actually experiencing God. But Jesus Himself rebuked the disciples after the resurrection for not believing the personal experiences of Mary Magdalene and the two disciples on the road to Emmaus (see Mark 16:9-14):

> *He rebuked their unbelief and hardness of heart, because they did not believe those who had seen Him after He had risen.* Mark 16:14

SUPERNATURAL

While it may not be wise to build doctrines on personal experience, it is equally unwise to totally disregard the experiences of other believers. God loves us, and He longs to reveal Himself to each of us in a very personal way. He said:

He who has My commandments and keeps them, it is he who loves Me. And he who loves Me will be loved by My Father, and I will love him and manifest Myself to him. John 14:21

The New Living Translation says it this way, *"I will reveal myself to each one of them."* Now that's personal!

To whom does God reveal Himself? To those who are in love with Him, not just with His Book.

Please don't misunderstand me. I love the Bible, I totally believe it from cover to cover, and I honor it as the Word of God. However, I'm more in love with the One Whom the Word reveals:

The Word became flesh and dwelt among us.
                                        John 1:14

It is one thing to be in love with a biography, but it is something totally and completely different to be in love with the one the biography discloses. The first is in the head, and the second is in the heart.

IS THAT A PERSONAL DAY?

Most personal experiences are just that—personal. They are often just for that particular individual at that precise moment. At other times, a personal experience may include a group gathering, a church or an entire move of God.

Although I don't make a hard ritual or rule about it, I often seek the presence of God in the early morning hours. After all, time spent with God is supposed to be a pleasure, not a problem. Most mornings I'm up anywhere from 1:00 to 4:00 AM spending time with God, and then I go back to bed and sleep.

For a period of time, I spent these night sessions seriously seeking Jesus to speak to me supernaturally (all of it is supernatural when you think about it) in any way He chose. I am a believer, therefore, my ears are open to His voice, and the voice of another I will not follow (see John 10:14). This led to an unusual experience:

GOD BLESS YOU!

I sat in my usual place in the dark waiting, worshipping and watching. Although there were no lights on in the room, I could still see the outlines of furniture. To my left, were several floor-length windows that looked out to a moonless back yard.

As I closed my eyes to surrender any distractions, to

my left I heard someone audibly sneeze. My first reaction was that someone in the house was up and was trying to sneak up on me. I opened my eyes and peered through the dimly outlined room, but there was no one there. There was absolutely no one and nothing between the window and me, three feet away.

"Perhaps I just imagined it," I thought. Maybe I just thought I'd heard someone sneeze. Then another thought occurred to me: *"Hmm, I wonder if angels sneeze?"*

My eyes were wide open now, and suddenly a flash of light went through the room. It was not a bright flash. It was more like the subtle flashes of lightening on a warm, humid summer evening in the South. I sat in the chair now, wondering if I had really seen what I thought I saw. Could it be that my blood pressure was up?

A few moments later there was another flash. Wow! I really didn't have a clue about what was going on. Then, as suddenly as it had begun, it ended, leaving me with lots of questions.

The next morning I shared my experience with Michelle. Then, I e-mailed Dan Duke (my spiritual father) and Gary Oates,[3] author of *Open My Eyes, Lord*, and asked them if they had ever heard of angels sneezing. They both replied that they had not.

At that point, I just placed the experience on the back burner, so to speak. Two weeks later Michelle came into my office one day to say, "I've got a verse for you whenever you get the time." Usually that means, "Now is a good time." So I opened my Bible to the verse she gave me. It was Job 41:18, and it said: *"His sneezings flash forth light."* Can you say, "That's unreal"? It was the confirmation I needed.

Now, to my brothers and sisters who would argue, "That's taken out of context," I would argue a *rhema* word in season is never out of context.

So what would be the purpose of angels sneezing? Who says there has to be a purpose for everything?

> *Then the LORD answered Job out of the whirlwind, and said:*
>
> *"Who is this who darkens counsel*
> *By words without knowledge?"*   Job 38:1-2

A loose (and contemporary) translation of that might be: "Why are you running your mouth as though you know something, when you really don't have a clue?"

Are we about to have a "sneezing revival"? Let's everyone snort some black pepper and ... SNEEZE ... PRAISE GOD, HALLELUJAH! (Hint: This is sarcasm.)

Is it possible that my hearing someone sneeze when no one was there could be the Father's way of saying, "I'm here with you"? That's what I believe personally, but I can't make a doctrine out of it. It was just a personal experience, meant just for me, and it was given by a personal God who loves me enough to let me know that He's with me.

SUPERNATURAL

I'll Take "This" ... But Not "That!"

Out of intimacy flows ministry to others. We deal more in detail with this subject in our book *The Power of Impartation*. It is in the secret place of prayer, worship and meditation that we become intimately acquainted with our Father, and thus learn how to be sensitive to the Holy Spirit.

Most of us have been taught that it is through much study, preparation and learning that ministry flows. There is much to gain from being a student of God's Word, and we certainly cannot and do not wish to discount that. However, the difference between releasing the Word with information and releasing the Word with power is intimacy with God. It is through intimacy that miracles, signs and wonders are released.

The Gospel is the power of God being released in signs and wonders when under the influence of the Holy Spirit (see Romans 15:19 and 1 Thessalonians 1:5). Therefore to diminish the role of the Holy Spirit is to limit His ability to flow through us.

Like it or not, you cannot separate the supernatural from an open heaven. Regardless of the semantics you place upon your cry for more of God-revival—an open heaven, signs and wonders, the miraculous, etc.—you cannot pick one and not the other. An open heaven isn't a buffet; it's a seven-course meal, with everything included for one price. That price was paid in full at Calvary, and the meal in question was extended to you and me through the resurrection and ascension of Christ.

Now, please read slowly and carefully the words of Paul's prayer for the church in Ephesus:

> *I pray for you constantly, asking God, the glorious Father of our Lord Jesus Christ, to give you spiritual wisdom and understanding, so that you might grow in your knowledge of God. I pray that your hearts will be flooded with light so that you can understand the wonderful future he has promised to those he called. I want you to realize what a rich and glorious inheritance he has given to his people. I pray that you will begin to understand the incredible greatness of his power for us who believe him. This is the same mighty power that raised Christ from the dead and seated him in the place of honor at God's right hand in the heavenly realms. Now he is far above any ruler or authority or power or leader or anything else in this world or in the world to come. And God has put all things under the authority of Christ, and he gave him this authority for the benefit of the church. And the church is his body; it is filled by Christ, who fills everything everywhere with his presence.*
> Ephesians 1:16-23, NLT

We can no longer afford to disbelieve God for the miraculous. It is His plan to equip the Church for end-time ministry with an unstoppable wave of signs and wonders, so that we can reap the final harvest. He set the standard, and the church has lowered it by hiding behind the doctrines of men and religious-sounding rhetoric in order to excuse their powerlessness. "Miracles are not for this dispensation," they say, but we cannot ignore this issue like a proverbial ostrich with its head in the sand. This issue will not go away. We must press in for the supernatural, even with all of the untidiness it is sure to bring.

The glory that will accompany the supernatural will far outweigh any hardship and criticism you may endure on your journey to these realms of Heaven on earth. One miracle will outshine all of the negativity that will come against you in your pursuit of an open heaven in your life, both personally and for your ministry.

For the Spirit-filled believer, the supernatural is already within you. Still, there is a progressive, lifelong quest for deeper waters of release around us and through us. Just when you think you've got it, the Lord weighs anchor, enticing us to follow deeper still. The extent to which you know the Christ within is the measure the heavens will be opened through you.

John Crowder, author and prophetic evangelist, writes, "The difference between worldly mysticism and Christian mysticism is that one seeks to discover the inner self, while the other seeks to discover the inner Christ— the very portal of Heaven."[4]

In the next chapter, we will delve into releasing Heaven's supernatural power in the marketplace, outside the confines of the church.

End Notes:
1. Cessationism: The belief that tongues, and other special gifts enjoyed by believers in the early Christian movement faded in the early fourth century CE, and are thus not present today. Definition courtesy of www.religioustolerance.org
2. Heresy hunters are self-appointed religious police who feel it is their responsibility to point out unorthodox practices, or doctrines, that do not conform to their personal opinion, preference or interpretation. They are generally anti-Charismatic in nature.
3. Gary Oates is a former pastor, author and conference speaker. www.garyoates.com
4. Crowder, John: *The New Mystics,* Shippensburg, PA (Destiny Image Publishers, Inc.: 2006
   John Crowder, "Sons of Thunder," www.thenewmystics.org

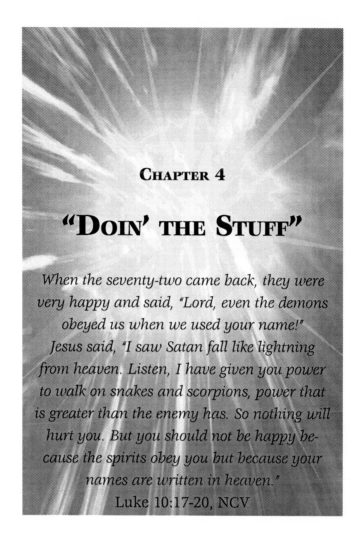

CHAPTER 4

"DOIN' THE STUFF"

When the seventy-two came back, they were very happy and said, "Lord, even the demons obeyed us when we used your name!" Jesus said, "I saw Satan fall like lightning from heaven. Listen, I have given you power to walk on snakes and scorpions, power that is greater than the enemy has. So nothing will hurt you. But you should not be happy because the spirits obey you but because your names are written in heaven."
Luke 10:17-20, NCV

The late John Wimber[1] used the phrase, "doin' the stuff," as meaning doing the things that Jesus did. Let's just assume for a moment that we really believe Jesus meant what He said, that we would do the works He did (see John 14:12). Do you realize how much fun it would be to do the "stuff" Jesus said we could do?

SUPERNATURAL

While Jesus did many miracles in church (that is, in the synagogue), He actually had more recorded miracles outside of that religious context. Miracles were not any more difficult or less difficult to do in one place than in the other. It was just that outside the synagogue (and Temple) He didn't have to deal with the arrogance of the Pharisees (although He did have the relatives to deal with). Some things never change.

Out Of the Closet

I was a closet Charismatic in the Baptist church for many years. I just didn't know that's what I was until revival hit our first church plant in 1994. Prior to that I had been a youth evangelist and an associate pastor in an independent Baptist church for several years. Like many former denominational ministers, I am both grateful and respective of my religious roots.

I received the baptism in the Holy Spirit as a teenager during the Charismatic Renewal in 1970. Following that experience, as I began to read the Scriptures, the Word of God became very much alive to me, and I struggled with what the Bible actually said versus what I had been told regarding miracles and healings having ceased.

Our church did follow the admonition of James. *"If there be any sick among you"* (KJV), we were to bring them before the church, anoint them with oil and pray over them in the name of the Lord (James 5:14-15). It just appeared to be more of a symbolic act than an actual belief that someone would really be healed. Somewhere we had missed that part about the *"prayer of faith"* would *"save the sick."* I'm not sure we knew we had verse 15 in our Bibles.

CAN YOU REPEAT THAT?

Many years later I was serving as an associate pastor when the parents of a teenage girl brought their daughter to the senior pastor for prayer. She had been in and out of the hospital since the age of six battling cancer. That week they had discovered a new large spot on her lung, clearly visible in the x-rays.

As one of the associate pastors, I, along with the deacons present, were asked to gather around, lay hands on her and pray. As I recall, the senior pastor anointed her with oil, then he turned to me and asked me to pray *"the prayer of faith."* The Holy Spirit suddenly rose up within me, and I cursed the cancer and commanded her to be healed.

That was about the extent of my brief prayer, but there seemed to be a stunned silence following. Some wondered if what I had said was really a proper prayer. What happened to the all-important "if it be Thy will" tag we always closed our prayers with? To be honest, I, too, was rather stunned by what had come out of my mouth.

After the service, I spoke with another associate and close friend about the prayer. He jokingly acknowledged that it had indeed been a little different from what we were accustomed to. And yet the following week we learned that new x-rays showed no trace of the tumor. To me, that was so cool! Now, that's doing the stuff!

I wish I could report that the girl lived happily ever after, but I can't. Within a couple of years, the cancer came back, and she passed away long before her time. We didn't know or understand then how to keep a miracle. This made clear to me the scriptural truth: *"my people are destroyed for lack of knowledge"* (Hosea 4:6). Nevertheless, I had seen the power of God at work, and there was no turning back.

OUT OF THE COMFORT ZONES

I will attempt to paraphrase a statement that pastor, author and revivalist Bill Johnson[2] made in a meeting I attended. "If Jesus did miracles as God in the flesh, I can admire them, but I am not required to do them. If however, He did them as a man anointed by the Holy Ghost, then I have an obligation to follow suit." Two things are crystal clear in this statement: (1) Jesus never would have made the statement He did in John 14:12 if it were not possible, and (2) This truth will work outside the confines of the church equally as well. For many people, including me, that's a preference.

It has been absolutely amazing to me to see how uncomfortable some Christians act when Jesus breaks out of the confines of the church. Some are even embarrassed to ask a blessing over their meal in public. Others, like Pharisees and relatives, are ready to faint if you ask someone if you could pray for them in the mall, or in most any other public place. I'm not talking about casting pearls before swine; I'm talking about being led specifically by the Holy Spirit to specific individuals in need and responding to that need.

I admire people like Patricia King[3] and others who purposely make efforts to bring the Gospel with signs and wonders to the unchurched. She writes in her book, *Light Belongs in the Darkness,*[4] "The power explosion seen on the streets during the day of Pentecost is the prototype for the emerging, last-days Church ... . We are on the verge of a new outpouring of the Spirit that will not be found inside of church buildings as much as it will be evidenced among the lost."

Is This a Good Time for You?

My willingness to obey God in this endeavor has not been without error. It requires constant listening for the Holy Spirit's voice, even when you don't feel like it. One such regrettable lesson follows.

Shortly after relocating to West Georgia, I was sitting on the front porch contentedly reading my Bible when my time with God was interrupted by one of the kids bringing me a phone call. Although the caller had asked specifically for me, I quickly realized it was nothing more than a sales call. God bless the people who do this for a living, and may they forgive me when they call my house. I was very polite that day as I listened to a lady attempting to sell me something to go along with our new Direct TV package. I told her, "Thanks, but no thanks."

As with most sales people, she didn't quit on the first refusal, but paused for a moment and then went to the next offer. For a second time, I told her, "No."

Not to be defeated, she paused again and offered me a third package. I laughed frustratingly, eager to get back to my reading, and once more I said more firmly, "No."

Yet again, there was a long pause, and then the lady finally hung up. The entire conversation had lasted about ten minutes, which is very unusual for me. I usually don't answer toll-free numbers, or, if I do, I ask the sales person to "hold a minute," and then I hand the phone to the cat and leave the room.

As soon as I set the phone down and picked up my Bible to continue my reading, the Holy Spirit spoke to me and said, "I had a word for her, and you weren't listening." I was stunned and tears welled up in my eyes. He continued, "She is a struggling single mom with a teenage son and daughter, trying to make ends meet. I had an encouraging word to her for you to deliver." And, for the second time, He said, "And you weren't listening!"

I was devastated. I wept and asked God for forgiveness. I then said to Him the thing most of us would have said under the circumstance: "Have her call back, and I'll do it." But she didn't call back, and I learned an unfortunate lesson the hard way.

The Calendar Says "It's Time For Revival"

Living in the supernatural realm is a 24/7 experience. Neither God, nor I, want miracles, signs and wonders only in the confines of the church. At this point in life, I cannot imagine anything else but living supernaturally. Yet, there are still many who believe that certain aspects of the supernatural are only supposed to happen within the confines of the church. It is humorous to me that when God actually does show up in church, it is often these same people who get upset about it.

After the renewal (as some prefer to call it) or revival (as I prefer to call it) hit in the mid 1990s, I was asked by a friend, who was filling an interim pastoral position in a rural Southern Baptist church, to come do a revival for him. Literally it was time for the "Annual 3rd-Week-of-August Revival." It seems, from the tradition of the church, that God was free that week each year to do whatever He pleased—or so most of us thought.

At the time, I was still a part of the Baptist denomination, and I knew I had to be careful regarding what I said and did. As the week began, things ran smoothly. I avoided any phrases or references to the baptism in the Spirit and His gifts. As the son of a Baptist pastor and, at the time, a Baptist pastor myself, I knew I had to be prudent. I focused only on those things we could agree on. I talked on God's power to save and His power to heal. After all, we Baptists did believe He could do it—whether we saw it or not.

SUPERNATURAL

By Thursday night of that week, I believed we had laid a strong enough foundation to ask if there was anyone sick who needed prayer. A man came forward with severe back pain and a crushed vertebrae. I looked at the congregation and asked them to join with me in prayer, believing for his healing. Smiling, they agreed and stretched their hands toward the man. I held my breath as I laid my hands on him and commanded his back to be healed.

DIDN'T YOU GET THE MEMO?

What happened next was the reason I was holding my breath. He "fell out" on the nice red carpet right in front of the altar. The bug-eyed members of the congregation slowly leaned forward in their pews to get a better view. Oops, I hadn't planned that far in advance. What explanation do you give someone who doesn't believe in such things or has never seen it happen?

I muttered something about *"He makes me lie down in green pastures"* while helping the man up, asking him if he felt any different? He replied that all the pain was gone as he bent over touching his toes. He was totally healed. The stunned audience seemed remarkably surprised and happy. Nevertheless, it seems one lady didn't get the memo regarding the 3rd-Week-of-August-Revival and God can do anything He wants.

Although I had never once purposely mentioned anything that would possibly offend my brothers, this sister was, without a doubt, offended. Unknown to the pastor and myself, she made quite a few phone calls the next day to other members to come stop this "mess."

On Friday night I walked naively through a basement door fellowship hall to find a circle of people joining hands in prayer. *"Great,"* I thought, *"I'll join them."* I walked right up, broke into the line and joined hands with the very sister who had called the meeting. God has a wonderful sense of humor.

So, it would appear, even God is confused at times about where and when He can work. Fortunately, we will never lack sincere brothers and sisters to help keep us on track. (Again, this is sarcasm.)

HERE'S YOUR SIGN

Consequently, how do we get the Kingdom to function outside a church building? The truth is that it isn't that difficult. It's as simple as 1, 2, 3:

1. Believe God isn't limited to anyone, anyplace or anything.
2. Sincerely have a desire to be used by God.
3. Listen and obey the promptings of the Holy Spirit.

Anyone can be used to give an encouraging word here or there. However, to be used by God in miracles, signs and wonders on a consistent basis, it is imperative to have been baptized in the Holy Spirit. That, within itself, is the empowerment zone for the entire Kingdom within us to be released (see Acts 1:8)

It is the manifestations of the Kingdom that cause unbelievers to sit up and take notice. (And, personally, it is much easier for me to minister to someone who is unchurched than to someone steeped in religion and tradition.) While the signs may differ from Old Testament Israel to us, still it is God's supernatural manifest presence that distinguishes us, the Church, from every other religion on earth.

In the list given above, if you believe 1 and 2, all you need be aware of is the Holy Spirit's leadings, and then obey them precisely. Some people think this is too easy. It is easy! He made it that way so that we could all do the works of Christ! However, you must do exactly what the Holy Spirit says, and you must do it when He says to do it. Nevertheless, if you miss it, as I did and have, He will give you another opportunity. His mercy endures forever. Hallelujah.

KNOWING THE MASTER OVER THE METHODS

Even so, in no way is this implied as a magical method, or a how-to formula. God wants relationship with His people, not routines and rituals. While it is this simple to walk in the supernatural, at the same time, the fastest way to close the heavens is to walk with unconfessed, known sin.

You don't have to bargain with Jesus to release His

glory through you. He has already made available to you everything you need to "do the stuff." You must realize it is His desire and plan to equip you completely, without lack in any area, to do His will. Get this down in your spirit. He is coming for a Bride whose body is in proportion to her Head. (Thank you Bill Johnson for that image!) Paul wrote:

> *And He put all things under His feet, and gave Him to be head over all things to the church, which is His body, the fullness of Him who fills all in all.* Ephesians 1:22-23

The opportunity to minister is available every time you walk out your door. The highways and byways of the marketplace provide unlimited openings to show that Jesus is Lord.

PROPHETIC EVANGELISM

Brady and Suzanne Burch often frequent a particular restaurant. The waitresses who work there have come to know that my friend Suzanne carries the word of the Lord in her mouth. Time after time, the Lord has used her to speak a word of comfort, encouragement and prophecy into their lives. Because of her faithfulness in the small things, the manager of the restaurant now recognizes her and often brings her prayer requests and opportunities to pray for others.

SUPERNATURAL

This type of prophetic evangelism is available to all of us, not just the "ministry men and women." Again, it is being sensitive, aware and available to hear, to speak and to do. Be committed to listen and obey, and the Holy Spirit will never lead you astray.

Whether it is a prophetic word, encouragement or laying hands on someone for healing, the gift that is available is the one needed at the moment. If someone broke a leg, an encouraging word is good, but a miracle is better. We might want to pray for the miracle, but only the Holy Spirit knows which gift will be received.

Equally important is being aware of your surroundings. What is the atmosphere conducive for? Is there a high level of faith present? Are there hindrances of doubt and unbelief present?

Timing can also play a role. Nevertheless, the Holy Spirit has all the answers. If He isn't saying anything, wait.

I'll close this chapter with an example of waiting on the Holy Spirit to move.

THE BEST RIBS IN TOWN

Michelle and I were going to pray for a close friend of ours who had been in a car accident. Ms. Catherine Dudrow at the time was eighty-eight years young, a real fire ball little lady, full of the Holy Ghost. She and her granddaughter had rear-ended another car, causing their air bags to deploy and hit Ms. Catherine in the chest, cracking several of her ribs. The doctors released her after deciding not to wrap her ribs for fear of pneumonia setting in, and this left her in acute pain every time she took a breath.

When we arrived at her home, she was seated at the kitchen table, along with her neighbor, who appeared to me to be in her mid-seventies. We were eager to pray for Ms. Catherine, but the Holy Spirit seemed to be saying, "Wait."

Small talk filled the room, mostly about the accident and resulting injuries. Finally the neighbor said, "Well, I had cracked ribs once, and there isn't anything you can do about it. It'll take six weeks before they quit hurting. That's just the way it is." It was obvious in that moment the reason for the delay. Even Jesus emptied the room of unbelief before raising Jairus' daughter from the dead.

During the course of the conversation, another of our close friends, Ralena Burgess, had joined us, having heard from God to come pray as well. Finally, the neighbor left the room to check on the granddaughter, and that's when I heard the Spirit saying, "Now!" Taking advantage of the opportunity, the very room became electric with our combined faith. I asked, "Ms. Catherine, do you want a miracle or a healing?"

She replied, "I want a miracle, but I'll take a healing."

I stood, taking her hand. Michelle placed her hand on the cracked ribs, and Ralena stood behind her. Then, I prayed: "In the name of Jesus, I command these cracked ribs to be healed and to go back into place, as they were before the accident!"

Ms. Catherine let out a sudden yelp, and Michelle screamed, "I felt them move back into place!" Ralena simply stood her ground with her hands raised in praise. Instantly the pain left, and our friend had her miracle. From the back room, both the granddaughter and the neighbor came rushing in to see what had happened.

Ms. Catherine turned to them and said, "I'm healed! Praise the Lord!" The neighbor stood speechless and watched. We then turned to the granddaughter, who had suffered a broken wrist in the accident and was unable to feel or move her fingers. After another quick prayer (actually a command), she began both to feel and to move her fingers and she was amazed.

At that point, I turned to the neighbor and asked her, "What kind of miracle do you need?" She took a step backward, threw up both her hands, and exclaimed, "I don't need nothing!" And I suppose that's exactly what she got that day.

Moving at the Speed of Spirit

Had we attempted to move on our own intuition in this case and not listened to what the Spirit was saying, no doubt the results would have been different. "Doing the stuff" is fun, especially when you realize that the supernatural goes with you wherever you go.

In the next two chapters, we will share experiences showing what fun the supernatural realm can be, but also showing how it can put the fear of the Lord in you.

End Notes:

1.John Wimber (born February 25, 1934 in Kirksville, Missouri, died November 17, 1997) was a charismatic pastor and one of the founding leaders of the Vineyard Movement. www.doin-the-stuff.com
2.Bill Johnson pastors Bethel Church in Redding, California. www.ibethel.org
3.Patricia King is an author, conference speaker and host of Extreme Prophetic TV. www.extremeprophetic.com
4.King, Patricia; *The Light Belongs in the Darkness,* Shippensburg, PA (Destiny Image Publishers: 2005)

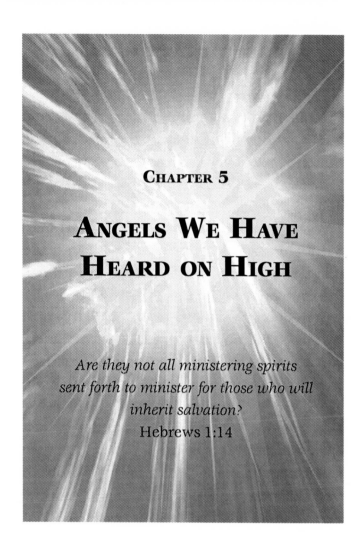

CHAPTER 5

ANGELS WE HAVE
HEARD ON HIGH

Are they not all ministering spirits
sent forth to minister for those who will
inherit salvation?
Hebrews 1:14

In July of 2006 we found ourselves finally moving to Bremen, Georgia, a small, rural town an hour west of Atlanta, just off of Interstate 20 and only minutes from the Alabama State line. We had survived fourteen long months of waiting for our former house to be sold.

In September of 2005, we had received a very detailed

prophetic word from Prophet Tim Mann[1] of Michigan. God was moving and repositioning us for specific reasons. The right location was imperative for the follow-through move of God. An open heaven for supernatural favor would follow—if we obeyed the precise geographical location.

I arose early on a warm and clear Tuesday morning, after a tiring move the day before. While the house was still quite, I stepped over boxes and made my way to the kitchen to prepare a well-deserved cappuccino. I sat down on our front porch to survey our new country surroundings. Across the road lay a picturesque setting of ninety-five acres (not ours ... yet) of gently rolling grass with a lake. In my mind, I thanked God that we had obeyed and had finally arrived at our destination. I slowly took a sip from my cup and said aloud, "Let the heavens be opened!"

Then, suddenly, there came a loud "Whoosh" sound, and every hair on my head, neck and arms stood up. Tears welled up in my tired eyes, as the presence of God became tangibly alive. I had the immediate awareness that angels were everywhere. The heavens were open.

TRAIN UP A CHILD

Unknown to me, from my early childhood there has been an unseen battle over my life. My very first memories revolve around eating a bottle of aspirin at eighteen months of age. I do not remember the hospital trip that followed.

At age three I fell into a ditch filled with water, with no one near to rescue me. Oddly, what I remember is thinking, "I can see underwater." I don't remember how I got out of the ditch, only that I later wondered how I'd done it.

My parents lost three of their children between my brother, who is ten years my senior, and myself. Doctors told my mother that it was doubtful I would survive either. But God ... !

My first encounters with the supernatural realm began with nightmares that started around the age of three or four. I never shared those nightmares with anyone. What could be expected from a child that young?

It all began with a recurring dream that something or someone was outside my bedroom window attempting to get inside. That "something" appeared to me as a black cloud with a face in it. I would awake from those nightmares terrified and afraid to move. It seemed that any sudden movement on my part might allow the "something" to come in and get me.

When my parents moved to the location where my mother still resides, I was four, and those dreams followed me. One night, as that recurring nightmare again attacked, I felt the dark presence at my window attempting to get into my bedroom. Then, suddenly, the room became bright with light. In the doorway stood a figure, brilliantly shining and illuminating the entire room with blinding light. I could not see a face, only a form. I was still petrified with fear, too afraid to move or make a sound. I awoke the next morning and considered that it was just part of the same dream. But something changed. I never again had another of those nightmares.

THE PROPHETIC VOICE

As the years passed I put it all out of my mind, considering it to have been nothing more than a dream. Then, in 1997, I attended a meeting where Prophet Kim Clement was speaking in Detroit, Michigan. The first night I thought it very odd that a thunderstorm had parked over the church where we were meeting. Throughout the night, peals of thunder could be heard over us.

When the meeting was over, I walked out to find my rental car and head back to the hotel. As I did, I looked up into the sky and saw that the stars were shining brightly. There wasn't a cloud in the sky. I thought to myself, *"Hmm, it must have cleared up awfully quick."*

The next night I met the pastor and asked him about the thunder. He smiled and said, "You heard it too?" He then began to tell me how not everyone hears what I heard. It was supernatural. Apparently it was heavenly warfare.

That night the prophet gave me a word, a word that awoke something in my spirit that had long since been forgotten, a word that would lead me into a destiny position. And that is God's ultimate goal, to lead us into our destiny positions. I include a portion of that prophetic word here because it relates directly to the supernatural events that are transpiring now, almost ten years later:

There is something inside of you that the devil tried to bury. There is something inside of you that you received as a young man. You don't even know this, but when you were just four years of age, I came into your house, and I visited you in the early hours of the morning. I came to you, and there was a frightening experience. But you saw something, and it is in your spirit. And this is the day that you are supposed to be alive. I'm going to give you a resurrection of truth, and as a result of it, you will see miracles that are going to take place a dime a dozen.[2]

OBEDIENCE — THE KEY TO THE PUZZLE

God has a calling, a destiny and a purpose for every soul that is born on the face of the earth. Unfortunately, so does Satan. We will fulfill one or the other:

"For I know the plans I have for you," says the LORD. "They are plans for good and not for disaster, to give you a future and a hope."
Jeremiah 29:11, NLT

The thief's purpose is to steal and kill and destroy. My purpose is to give life in all its fullness.
John 10:10, NLT

Here we see two very distinct and clear plans for every life. One is for good, and the other is for destruction. Obedience to God determines whether we completely, or partially, fulfill His plan for our lives. If we want God's best, then we must obey in the smallest details—whether we understand them or not. If we are determined to take nothing less than God's best, then He clearly and accurately speaks to us to accomplish His greater purposes.

We must understand: while we are just a piece of the puzzle in God's Kingdom, He sees the whole, not just that one part. But our part completes the whole. The Kingdom is global, but my portion is just a small piece of that whole.

For us to personally position ourselves at a specific and strategic location for a supernatural outpouring required that we obey fully something that we did not yet understand. We knew that God had said, "Move!" The question was: To where?

Over a period of seventeen months, we looked at thirty-one houses between Rome and LaGrange, Georgia. One by one, God closed the door to the houses that were not in His perfect plan, because we had yielded our will to fully obey, and we would settle for nothing less.

For reasons too many to mention, from timing to location, we carefully avoided what could have been partial obedience to obtain complete obedience. Through specific and detailed prophetic words, dreams and Holy Spirit leading, we have now found an open portal within us, upon us and over us. You can't beat that combination! This is an open heaven.

MEANWHILE, BACK AT THE RANCH

Shortly after moving in, one Sunday afternoon we were having a service in our new house. Several of our friends had joined us to soak in God's presence. As I was preparing to minister at the keyboard, a heavy, weighty presence entered the room, and the tangible glory of the Lord filled the atmosphere.

I felt an intense angelic presence to my left beside my keyboard. We waited in the stillness of the holy hush, until one of our gifted prophetic intercessors cried out in a loud voice, "There's a huge angel standing there (pointing to my keyboard position). He said his name is Breakthrough, and he's here to release a breakthrough in this place!"

It was as though a Holy Ghost bomb had gone off in that room. People were moaning, falling on the floor, unable to stand, because of the weightiness of God's presence. His blanket covered the room, and we were nothing more than "toast" for a couple of hours.

It was hours later before we could again communicate with any natural sensibility. Then, from around the room, the comments came. Some had literally seen the angel, others had seen a bright light, but all had felt his presence.

Often God sends an announcement through such an angelic visitation of things He is about to do. Clearly, this particular announcement is one we have been waiting for.

The dreams, visions, plans and purposes of God often

take years to fulfill. Humanly speaking, we receive a prophetic word one day and expect the fulfillment of it the next. However, in between the decree and the fulfillment, more times than not, lies a process of spiritual alignment to complete God's bigger purposes.

Many times there are multiple factors on different fronts needed to execute one decree of God. It can range from the season, the timing and the location, to obedience or disobedience. Once the components come together, then the whole can be accomplished, keeping in mind that we are just a piece in God's Kingdom puzzle.

We had no idea, when we followed God in our move from the northern suburbs of Atlanta west to the Georgia-Alabama line, what was in store for us. We had neither friends, relatives or acquaintances in the area. We knew nothing whatsoever about Bremen, Georgia, except that the pieces of our personal puzzle had clearly and undeniably aligned.

The angelic activity surrounding our home and land is unlike anything I've felt in years. The consciousness and constant awareness of their presence it truly astounding. Encounters come almost on a daily basis. Just so you can get an idea, I will list a few that stand out.

Is That for Me?

One night my wife and I had just gone to bed. Both of us were very tired and sleepy. Suddenly I sensed the presence of a different angel standing by the bed with something in his hand. I told Michelle about the angel, adding, "You're not going to believe what's in his hand." But, before I could tell her what it was, we both fell fast asleep.

During the course of the night, I had what I call "God dreams." There were two of them, and they were very detailed. This is a kind of night vision in which God simply speaks directly Spirit to spirit. Both of these dreams directly relayed information that we needed at the time. When I awoke and told Michelle about the dreams, I was then able to tell her what had been in the angel's hand ... a cell phone.

A cell phone? What does an angel need with a cell phone? I could think of nothing. Then I realized what it represented: "I have something to communicate to you." Through those two dreams, God spoke directly to my spirit man. We've had several more "God dreams" since then, but I haven't seen any more angels with cell phones.

As Long as You're in There ...

Since the time our first grandson learned that his two feet could actually carry him places, like room to room, he hasn't stopped moving. Actually he runs. He only stops running to eat or sleep. If he's moving, he's running.

One day, while visiting Mom-Mom and Paw-Paw, he ran into the kitchen to look for some cookies, and we could clearly see him from the next room. While we continued to have a conversation with his mother (my daughter), he suddenly screamed in a panic and ran back to where we were with tears in his eyes. He kept looking back into the kitchen and then back at us. It was clear that he had seen something.

We jokingly said, "It must have been our kitchen angel." Nevertheless he wouldn't return to the kitchen anymore that day unless we went with him.

We were serious about that kitchen angel. On several occasions, both Michelle and I have witnessed an angel's presence in that area of the house. Who's to say for sure that it's always the same angel, but we dubbed him our kitchen angel.

WHAT'S WITH THE ORBS?

A lot of information can be found on the Internet these days regarding what many are calling "angelic orbs." An *orb* simply means "a sphere, something round in circumference." Please keep in mind that not everything you read on the Internet is true or biblical. Most of it certainly isn't.

Still, we began to notice some orbs in pictures we would take around the house, in both ministry and non-ministry settings. This prompted my curiosity—to say the very least. Some "googling" placed me at a site containing some 17th- and 18th-century religious paintings, and among them were paintings of angels holding orbs in their hands. What, I wondered, would have prompted the artist to paint those round spheres in the angel's hands?

At one of our ministry gathering times in our home, several of us were sitting in our family room discussing the orbs. Suddenly my eyes were opened to see two orbs around one of our intercessors. I ran to get my camera and quickly took a photo. The digital camera displayed the orbs exactly as I was seeing them in the natural.

My theory is that these orbs represent the spiritual beings in a pre-manifested state. If that theory holds true, it could also represent the demonic side as well. This is not a dogmatic, unbendable, nonnegotiable, argumentative truth. It merely represents a possibility.

During the healing revival of the late 1940s and early 1950s, William Branham would wait until an angel appeared to him before he would start ministering to the people. Often he saw this angel as an orb—although that wasn't the terminology he used:

> When the angel of the Lord came down into a meeting, Bill felt a distinctively holy presence that made his flesh tingle as though the air was charged with electrical energy. Often Bill saw the angel of the Lord in his meetings looking like a bubble of light hanging in the air a few feet away from him.[3]

A "bubble of light hanging in the air" sounds like an orb to me.

These heavenly messengers are not present to make us feel good or to entertain us; they, too, are here for a purpose:

SUPERNATURAL

Are they not all ministering spirits sent forth to minister for those who will inherit salvation?
Hebrews 1:14

Angels play an important role in opening the heavens over us, around us and through us. The very idea of an open heaven in scripture is conceived as a gateway for the supernatural of Heaven to invade earth.

WHAT GOES UP ...

Genesis reveals Jacob's dream and his revelation that followed:

Then he dreamed, and behold, a ladder was set up on the earth, and its top reached to heaven; and there the angels of God were ascending and descending on it ... .
And he was afraid and said, "How awesome is this place! This is none other than the house of God, and this is the gate of heaven!"
Genesis 28:12 and 17

Regardless of your theological position, the angelic host is among us. We will only see and hear of ever-increasing visitations by them in the coming days, for they play an important role in advancing the Kingdom of God. Understanding that this Kingdom is being advanced through us will bring more supernatural encounters with the angelic hosts.

We don't seek angels. However, we must recognize them as messengers from Heaven sent to aid, protect and assist us in fulfilling our calling, our purpose and our destiny. When the heavens are open, angels are actively engaged in releasing Kingdom purposes within us and upon those to whom we minister.

In fact, Jesus told Nathaniel to expect to see an increase of such supernatural situations:

> *Jesus asked him, "Do you believe all this just because I told you I had seen you under the fig tree? You will see greater things than this." Then he said, "The truth is, you will all see heaven open and the angels of God going up and down upon the Son of Man."* John 1:50-51., NLT

I believe these words are applicable today as well. You must understand: we do not consider ourselves something special or super-spiritual, nevertheless, we do expect and anticipate the heavenly hosts to work alongside us in accomplishing God's will *"on earth, as it is in heaven."*

As we acknowledge and pursue the Holy Spirit to reveal and expand our abilities to perceive the supernatural, we should naturally expect the angelic ones to be a part of that function. We usually get what we're expecting, so expect the supernatural.

SUPERNATURAL

End Notes:

1. Tim Mann can be reached through Harvest Fire International, Grand Rapids, Michigan. www.hfi-online.com
2. A prophetic word given by Kim Clement to Eddie Rogers 8-23-97 in Detroit, Michigan. Kim Clement, www.kimclement.com
3. Jorgensen, Owen; *Supernatural: The Life of William Branham,* Book 3, pg 126. (While we admire the humility and gifting that was upon this man of God, we do not endorse the teachings of his latter years.)

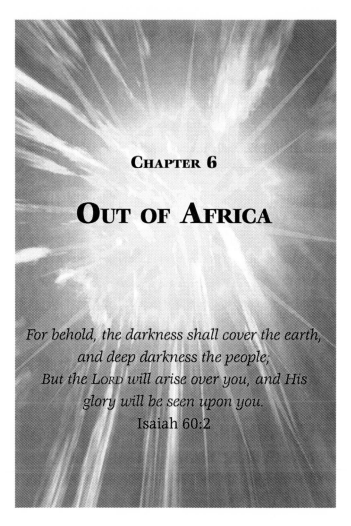

CHAPTER 6

OUT OF AFRICA

For behold, the darkness shall cover the earth,
and deep darkness the people;
But the LORD will arise over you, and His
glory will be seen upon you.
Isaiah 60:2

Shortly after our move, I was speaking with a good friend, Pastor Marc Lawson,[1] by telephone one day, and he asked me, "Have you heard of T.B. Joshua?" I told him I had heard the name but knew nothing about the man.

Marc replied, "You've got to see this guy. He stretches his hand toward people, and tumors, cancer and other stuff are just obliterated."

"Hmmm, my kind of guy," I thought.

After another quick "Google" search, I was watching Emmanuel TV, "The Synagogue Church of All Nations" television programming, featuring Prophet T.B. Joshua.[2] For three straight days I sat and watched in amazement. I left it on day and night. I wanted the anointing emanating from Lagos, Nigeria, to flood our home.

Never have I witnessed the raw power of God demonstrated in such a manner. I have been blessed to witness in person blind eyes open, the deaf hear and the lame walk, but never have I seen such authority and power as this.

SETTING THE STANDARD

I watched a tape of a man lying in the back seat of a car driven to the church for healing. X-rays clearly showed that he had two broken legs, clean breaks, severing the femur bones in half. The man of God never touched him physically. In the Spirit, he simply stretched his hands toward the man. Then both legs began to jump and shake, as an unseen hand supernaturally mended the bones together. It all happened in what appeared to be about five minutes time.

Then the man stood up and walked, to the cheers of people from around the world who had come to witness the miracles that are transpiring in that place. The praise all went to Jesus. The man, T.B. Joshua, is both prophet and miracle worker, yet he walks with great humility of spirit. There is a valuable lesson to be learned here.

It wasn't just the amazing miracles that impressed me; it was the amazing deliverances as well. In one session, an obviously deranged man stood several feet from the man of God, challenging him by growling and shaking his fist. Prophet Joshua grinned as though he were playing a game of cat and mouse. With hands on his hips, he lifted one leg, as if swatting an imaginary soccer ball to the side. Ten feet away, the possessed man's legs went out from under him. Shocked, he attempted to crawl over to a chair to pull himself up. As he did this, Prophet Joshua stretched his hand toward him and waved his hand back toward the middle of the aisle. Unseen hands grabbed the man by the feet and pulled him back to where he had once been standing. In disbelief and disgust, the man shook his head. Moments later, he was giving glory to God for his deliverance.

As I sat in front of my computer, watching miracle after miracle, the Holy Spirit spoke to me in an almost audible voice. I was stunned at what I heard: "This is the standard I've set for My Church." God doesn't want us satisfied merely believing that this is a possibility that someone might achieve; He wants every one of us living in the reality of this truth. These miracles I witnessed and the voice of the Lord saying, "This is the standard" (and not the exception) lifted my faith to say, "I can do that too."

There was a direct correlation in seeing those broken bones mend and the lifting of my faith to pray for Ms.

Catherine's cracked ribs to instantly mend. I knew that I knew that I knew that she would be miraculously healed—because my faith had been raised to a new level.

"DARK" IS RELATIVE

Africa, for centuries now, has been called "the dark continent." This was not without reason. High levels of witchcraft have dominated the landscape. Western culture is truly ignorant when it comes to the reality of such demonic forces, and yet God is raising up, across the backdrop of that "dark" continent, men and women who walk in holiness and power, which truly decimates the powers of the enemy.

In a television interview with Sid Roth,[3] on his program "It's Supernatural," Pastor Robert Kayanja of Uganda tells of a confrontation with a witch doctor. The witch doctor told him that if he didn't stop his ministry and leave the area, within three days he would be "a dead man."

The Spirit of God rose up in Robert, and he responded boldly, "No! Unless you repent, it will be you who is dead within three days."

Three days later Pastor Robert and his co-workers were worshipping and praising the Lord in his house at exactly the time the witch doctor had told him he would die. Outside the house, they heard a loud noise like a car crashing. They rushed out and gathered on the street with others who had heard the same sound. There was no sign of an accident, but lying in the middle of the road was the witch doctor's body, and his severed head was lying apart near the ditch.

What happened? It's simple. An angel of the Lord stood his ground to protect the man of God. It is unwise to think these things are fairy tales. They are a living reality to those who know and embrace the truth. It is foolish to think of them as mere fables or to discount them as superstition. When faced with the threats of Satan, we'd better be able to say with Paul, *"My words didn't come to you in the wisdom of men, but in the power of God."*[4]

In his book, *The Witchdoctor and the Man,*[5] a fourth generation, high-level witchdoctor, Samuel Vagalas Kanco, describes in great detail his involvement in the occult. He was supernaturally saved and delivered when Jesus appeared to him and told him to inform the church regarding the reality of these events.

Dr. Pat Holliday,[6] co-author of the book, told me in a phone interview that while visiting Bishop Kancos' church in Accra, Ghana, she witnessed direct clashes between darkness and light. While some think deliverance ministry is a specialty, in Africa it is just another part of everyday Kingdom work, along with miracles, healing and salvation.

I heard one African evangelist say, regarding Western culture's seeming disbelief in the supernatural realm, "What you have is educated unbelief." To walk in the supernatural we must embrace the fact that there is both good and evil.

Again, drawing from our illustration of a smorgasbord buffet, it isn't pick and choose. And neither are we to feel overwhelmed at the power of the dark side. This isn't "Star Wars"; it's Heart Wars. Whom will you serve? All power and authority belong to Christ, and the ability to wield this power and authority has been given to His Church.[7] It is time for His Church to walk forward in fullness of power, not limping behind with irrelevant doctrines that left all power with the first-century church.

Bishop Kanco tells the story of some American missionaries who went into a village without the power of the Holy Spirit. The enemy they thought they were confronting was one of superstition. The witches of the village quickly oppressed them with a demon of madness after the missionaries demolished one of their occultic altars. Fortunately for the missionaries, the local police recognized the madness as demonic and called Bishop Kanco to come to the jail and deliver these men from witchcraft. After that episode, you can be sure these men reevaluated their doctrinal positions to find the power of Jesus a living reality before attempting something so foolish again.

WILLY, THE KILLER WHALE

Here in America, we counsel and drug our demons rather than cast them out. Once, while ministering in a church in South Georgia, three elders called me into a room where they were holding a very large, angry man. He stood well over six and a half feet tall, and weighed probably three hundred and fifty pounds. They called him Free Willy, after the movie of the same name.

While undeniably as big as a whale, one thing was for sure: Willy wasn't free. An elder held each arm, and another brother was behind him, attempting to put his arms around that massive waist. As I entered the room, I saw two red dots looking through this man's pupils. When I approached him, he said to me, "I'm gonna kill you."

I replied, "Not today, you're not!"

At that response, he quickly lunged toward me, dragging the elders in tow. I closed my eyes and lifted one hand in front of me and simply said, "Jesus." I felt a literal wind come from behind me, as Willy's substantial chest touched my outstretched hand. I opened my eyes in time to see Willy (and the elders holding him) knocked ten feet backward into the wall behind them. Willy slid slowly down the wall. It was as if he had been hit with a 2" x 4" in the forehead.

Not wanting to miss my opportunity, I jumped squarely in the middle of his large belly and commanded the demon to come out. Not long afterward, Willy was indeed free.

READY OR NOT ...

We are living in a day when we cannot compromise our Christian walk by tolerating any form of sin in our lives. There is too much at stake. God's Kingdom is one of power, and those who live daily in a fresh baptism of His blood and anointing will see the fruit of their labor:

SUPERNATURAL

For the Kingdom of God is not just fancy talk; it is living by God's power.

1 Corinthians 4:20, NLT

When confronted by the enemy's power, you don't have time for a quick trip to the confessional. This is why we are to live a habitual life-style of holiness, prayer and fasting. When Jesus said, *"This kind doesn't go out but by prayer and fasting,"* He didn't mean go take three days off and then come back. He meant that our life-style should be one that reflects seeking Him on an ongoing basis.

The men of God from Africa live in the supernatural daily, unlike most Americans, who's idea of the supernatural may be an hour on Sunday morning. It would be wonderful if we could get all the power we need in one hour each week, but it's not possible. Communion with God must be moment by moment.

THE GOSPEL IN BLACK AND WHITE

South African Rodney Howard-Browne[8] calls himself a missionary to America, and indeed he is. Often, when we think of Africans, we only think of black Africans, forgetting that there are white Africans as well. Rodney and his wife came here from the nation of South Africa, and I can honestly say that I have been around few individuals who carry the tangible presence of God like this man. This may be true partly because we have learned to recognize those who carry an impartation we can draw from, but I believe it is primarily because he is experienced in the supernatural realms of God. You can only deliver the goods you have:

> *But Peter said, "I don't have any money for you. But I'll give you what I have. In the name of Jesus Christ of Nazareth, get up and walk!"*
>
> Acts 3:6, NLT

At a New Year's Eve service at The River at Tampa Bay Church in 2006, Rodney prayed for Michelle, my wife. Actually, he barely touched her. After the service was over, I had to literally carry her to the car. Then I had to carry her into our hotel and put her in the bed. I wish you could have seen the look on the receptionist's face as we passed through the lobby (keeping in mind that it was New Year's Eve)! These natural bodies are only capable of handling so much from the other realm. That's why we will need a new and glorified body to stand eternally in God's presence.

Dr. Elijah Maswanganyi[9] is another highly educated South African who moves in the supernatural. I met Elijah at a conference in the late 1990s. I sat in awe and wept as I listened to the stories of miracles, healings and even the raising of the dead. I felt as though I was sitting at the feet of the apostles, listening to the book of Acts relived.

After the meeting was over, I waited in line just to shake his hand. I was so hungry for more of what I had heard, hungry to experience it. When my turn came, I told him how I longed for more of the supernatural realms of God, but I wasn't expecting what came next. In his heavy-accented English, this great man of faith said to me, "Every nation I go to, God shows me one man to release my anointing upon, and you are that man."

He then got down on his knees and laid his hands on my feet and began to pray. He prayed for all the nations that I would go to, as well as for the glory of God to be released. I was humbled and wept as I felt as though I was being enveloped in liquid fire and love. It was inde-scribable. And yes, there was immediate increase in awareness of the supernatural realm. (We discuss more about this kind of impartation in our book, *The Power of Impartation*.[10])

Like Prophet T.B. Joshua, Elijah Maswanganyi is also a man who is filled, not only with the power of Heaven, but also with a great love and humility of spirit.

WALK SOFTLY AND CARRY A BIG HOLY GHOST!

Jesus taught:

Blessed are the poor in spirit, for theirs is the kingdom of heaven.   Matthew 5:3

"Poor in spirit" is a reference to a humble recognition and dependence upon God for His breakthrough anoint-ing. As the clashes between God's servants and demonic

powers intensify, there must be a greater reliance upon the Holy Spirit and the angelic hosts to set captives free.

Never has there been a time to walk more uprightly in spirit than now. If our eyes could penetrate the veil of the supernatural we would clearly see the hotly contested battle over the souls of men. The enemy's demonic hordes are looking for every opportunity to destroy the children of God—especially His ministers.

Whether it is nationally or locally, every time a servant of God falls to the enemy's tactics, the Kingdom of God suffers. According to Bishop Kanco, it is only when a Christian continually acts out unrepentant sin that they become vulnerable to Satan's snares. A hedge of fire and guardian angels wielding their swords supernaturally protects Spirit-filled believers who are walking in purity of heart without hidden sin.

I would think it wise to heed the warning of these men of God who know firsthand the strategies of demons. When a word of warning comes our way by the Holy Spirit and we don't heed it, we are only asking for a fall. Too much is at stake to turn a blind eye to the dark side, as if ignoring it will make it go away.

In love, I confronted an ordained minister regarding the pornographic demon of lust I saw upon him. While I loved the man, I actually felt dirty in his presence. He acknowledged to me in private that it was true, but he was not willing to go through an embarrassing deliverance session. He told me that he had the problem "fifty percent under control." That meant he was also under fifty percent demonic control. I wouldn't have cared if he had it ninety-nine percent under control. Who wants one percent of a demon?

The real problem lies in the fact that most ministers are unaccountable to anyone. Because of this, they have no one to confide in who holds both their best interest and the Kingdom of Heaven at heart. Still, too much of the Body of Christ becomes judgmental and critical at the fall of a Christian brother or sister. If we are a hundred percent under the Holy Spirit's control and power, it will be the enemy fleeing from us and not us from him.

ANOTHER FLY-BY-NIGHT OPERATION

Ron Ssali, an apostle from Uganda, Africa, tells of a threat from a witchdoctor upon his life. One night he literally saw the witchdoctor flying on a goat skin at a high rate of speed, coming directly toward him. With little time to react, he threw his hand toward the demonically possessed man and said, "In the name of Jesus, change your direction!" Immediately the power of God knocked the man to the ground, and he ran away as fast as he could.[11]

The power of the enemy is real, but the power of Jesus Christ is greater. There is no comparison. Nevertheless, if you don't possess the One, you will fall for the other.

If we are going to walk in the supernatural, we must be aware that wrapped together in the one realm is both good and evil. If you pursue the glory of God, you can expect interference from the other. Just don't fear it. Take authority over it. The enemy knows whether or not you are aware that you have authority over him.

GENUINE OR IMITATION?

Once, while ministering at a church in Memphis, Tennessee, the pastor informed us that a warlock had come to disrupt the meeting. Expecting the worse, we prayed and bound any hindrances prior to the service.

At the close of the service, I found myself looking at what appeared to be an eighteen- or nineteen-year-old young man, but he was dressed all in black, with dyed black hair and black eyeliner. I laid my hands on his head, and he fell out under the power of God. As I knelt down beside him, the Holy Spirit said to me, "He's clean. He's just looking for attention."

I sat him up, and we talked. He was indeed just a lonely kid looking for attention. I led him in a prayer of salvation, and his countenance changed dramatically. One thing you can be sure of: even though he was pretending to be what he was not, demon forces were already poised to bring him into the genuine.

HOLINESS IS A COMMAND, NOT AN OPTION

We must walk in integrity of truth and spirit. When confronted with the demonic realm, that isn't the time to decide to walk in holiness of character. Character is a choice, which hopefully has already been made. Holiness, in fact, is a command. God has said emphatically:

Be holy, for I am holy.   1 Peter 1:16

The standard was initially set in Jesus, and those who have followed in His footsteps without excuse are among us today. If His standard is being lived out, even by one of us, then it is available to all of us. Let us pursue with diligence and patience the reality of this realm of glory, no matter where it leads us.

BLINDED BY THE LIGHT

"The glory of this latter temple shall be greater than the former," says the LORD of hosts.

Haggai 2:9

As the manifest presence of Jesus increases, the more confrontations between light and dark we will see. Light exposes darkness. Demons prefer to hide, but when the anointing of God becomes strong, they unwittingly expose themselves.

When the demonically oppressed came into Jesus' presence in His day, His time on the earth, they would cry out. The Light blinded them. The only thing that has changed since then is our ability to produce the levels of anointing to expose them. The good news is this: It's still His day!

As we learn to walk in the supernatural, it will be the greater glory in us which will produce the same results as Jesus had in His day or any of our brothers from Africa have today. I wholeheartedly believe that our ability to continually increase in all things supernatural is directly proportionate to our ongoing love affair with Jesus. He must be preeminent above all things in us and work all things through us. This cannot be a religious ritual, but must become an ongoing intimate relationship.

I have heard many speak of certain ministers and say, "I wish I had their anointing." Unfortunately, most have failed to consider the price involved to get them to that same level of power with God.

Several months after hearing the Holy Spirit speak to me regarding "the standard" of power He has set for the Church, He spoke to me again. This time I was walking along a prayer trail that crosses our property, and I was praying as I walked. My thoughts returned to the demonstration of power I had witness on Prophet T.B. Joshua. While I know very little about the man personally, I have been through enough in the last twenty years of ministry to know that it is often in the secluded, or hidden, places of the Spirit that the greatest release of His power and presence is made known. It is in the secret place, that place that no one else will ever see, where Jesus empties us of selfish ambitions and dreams and fills us with His purpose and destiny. This is not just for our sake, but rather for His glory and the sake of others.

So what was the word the Holy Spirit lovingly whispered in my ear that day on the prayer trail? He said, "Allow Me to do in you what I did in him, and I will release through you what I released in him."

Does it seem strange that the Holy Spirit would ask for my permission? Not at all. To better understand this, I close with a quote from author and minister Myles Munroe. "Why is this so important to understand? Because God is a spirit, and when He speaks, His words become law. His integrity will not permit Him to violate or break His word; therefore, whatever He speaks becomes a law even unto God. He will never break His word nor violate His principles.

"In this case, the result is that God, in His sovereignty, has decided to delegate authority and dominion in the earth to mankind—a spirit in a body. This is why God cannot do anything on earth without the cooperation of a human. Man is God's legal agency and access to earth.

"God is and remains absolutely sovereign, but He has chosen to limit His activity or intervention on the earth to that which we, the proprietors, give Him permission to do. The way we grant that permission is through prayer."[12]

An Admiral in the Navy, though he outranks the commanding officer of a vessel, will ask permission to come aboard. He will then patiently wait until the officer in charge of that ship grants him permission to come on board and has relinquished his command to the higher-ranking Admiral. When the Holy Spirit asks permission to "come on board," while the choice is still ours to make, what other reply can we give but, "Permission granted"?

End Notes:

1. Marc Lawson is pastor of North Gate Church of Atlanta, Woodstock, Georgia. www.ngca.org

2. Prophet T.B. Joshua, Emmanuel TV and The Synagogue Church of All Nations can be accessed via http://scoan.org/

3. Sid Roth, http://sidroth.org, Robert Kayanja footage via "It's Supernatural" archives, 2003. Robert Kayanja Ministries, http://www.kayanja.org/abouts/calling.htm

4. 1 Corinthians 2:4, My paraphrase

5. Kanco, Samuel Vagalas; *The Witchdoctor and the Man-Fourth Generation Witchdoctor Finds Christ.* Jacksonville, Florida (Agape Publishers: 2000.) An e-book is available through http://www.agapepublishers.com/
   The information on Bishop Kanco is taken from http://www.hand2handministry.com/R-3.html, May 2007

6. Pat Holliday, Ph.D. http://patholliday.com/index.html

7. See Matthew 28:18 and Ephesians 1:20-23

8. Rodney Howard-Browne is an author, Senior Pastor of The River @ Tampa Bay, Florida and international crusade revivalist, http://revival.com

9. Dr. Elijah Maswanganyi is an international motivational speaker from South Africa, author of twenty-seven books, known as the "Billy Graham" of Africa; A graduate of SAST SA, Haggai Institute Singapore and Fuller University USA. Recipient of twenty-four awards worldwide, including inclusion in Who's Who in the World, Volume 13 of 1996. He has traveled to a hundred and thirty-three countries worldwide.

10. Rogers, Eddie T.; *The Power of Impartation: The Need For Divine Appointments with Spiritual Fathers*; Greenwell Springs, Louisiana (McDougal & Associates: 2006)

11. Ron Ssali information ibid Sid Roth. "It's Supernatural" archive 2003

12. Munroe, Myles; *Rediscovering the Kingdom*; Shippensburg, PA. (Destiny Image Publishers: 2004)
    Myles Munroe, Bahamas Faith Ministries International, www.bfmmm.com

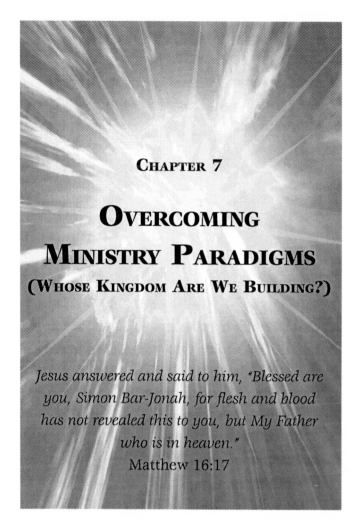

CHAPTER 7

OVERCOMING MINISTRY PARADIGMS
(WHOSE KINGDOM ARE WE BUILDING?)

Jesus answered and said to him, "Blessed are you, Simon Bar-Jonah, for flesh and blood has not revealed this to you, but My Father who is in heaven."
Matthew 16:17

I love being challenged in my thinking regarding the things of the Spirit. I never want to fall into a category of those who feel, "Oh, I already know that." The things the Holy Spirit is revealing to us today are unprecedented. Some would argue, "There's nothing new under the sun." Unfortunately, I haven't met any Solomons lately.

God said through Isaiah:

SUPERNATURAL

For precept must be upon precept, precept upon precept, Line upon line, line upon line, Here a little, there a little.   Isaiah 28:10

To Tell the Truth

Truth is revealed to us, the Church, in layers. We are carried *"from glory to glory"* (2 Corinthians 3:18). Martin Luther rediscovered justification by faith, not works. At the turn of the twentieth century, the Church rediscovered the baptism of the Spirit. In the 1980s we rediscovered the fact that God not only called prophets; He apparently still spoke through them. Now we are embracing the apostolic office and other new ideas, like churches in houses, office parks, theatres and even in the street.

These are pieces to a greater whole, that is, the Kingdom of God in power through individuals (with and without seminary degrees). God's big picture involves bringing together the Church globally, not just a church locally—although His Church is made up of local churches. To borrow a concept from John Alley's book, *The Apostolic Revelation: The Reformation of the Church*,[1] in each city, there is only one church, the Church of the Lord Jesus Christ. Although it may be fragmented into many different denominations, non-denominations, traditional and Spirit-filled bodies, it still remains one Church, and Jesus will return for His Church.

God ordains and gifts certain individuals in five-fold ministry offices to function together to accomplish the whole. Some will be gifted to a single body of believers, others to regions, territories or nations. To some, God will even give a global voice. However, it will always be building upon the former. When we hear something "new," therefore, we must not always say, "I can't believe that because I've never heard it before." At some point, everything we heard was new. At least, it was new to us.

A CALL FOR WISDOM

I'm not saying I believe everything that comes down the pike is from God. What I'm saying is that we must use the wisdom of the Berean church and search the Scriptures to see if these things are so (see Acts 17:10-11). When you cannot find chapter and verse to fit your idea, remember that we have the Holy Spirit. He will guide us into all truth (see John 16:13). Test the spirit and see if it is of God (see 1 John 4:1). His sheep recognize His voice (see John 10:4-5). Simply put, don't automatically consider a new concept to be wrong or irrelevant simply because you haven't personally experienced it yet.

The Holy Spirit isn't removing truth from the earth, but is, rather, constantly adding to the truth we already have. For example, the Mosaic covenant brought with it forgiveness of sin through the sacrifice of animals. That was true. Today, however, we have a better covenant, and the forgiveness of sins through the sacrifice of Jesus Christ (see Hebrews 8:6). The first was a truth, but this is an even greater truth.

SUPERNATURAL

When we cease to build upon revealed truth, we have ceased to build God's Kingdom purposes. His is an eternal Kingdom, revealing eternal truths in progressive succession, whereby His Kingdom policies are enforced in an ever-expanding capacity.

WHO YA GONNA CALL?

Twenty years ago, when I first answered the call to the ministry, the only people raised from the dead I was familiar with were those recorded in the Bible. Today we hear and know of people being raised from the dead in India, Africa, China, South America and Mexico.

My friend, Mel Bond,[2] pastors a church near St. Louis, Missouri. A few years ago, he was called to the hospital where a family member of someone in his church had just died. Standing in the hallway outside the room where this person had just been pronounced dead by the attending physician were the doctor, nurses and weeping family members, already beginning to plan a funeral.

He asked permission to step into the room and pray, and they acknowledged that he could. A few minutes later, he stepped back into the hallway and told the still-weeping family that there was no need to plan a funeral. The disbelieving physician and family members shot past him into the room to find the former corpse sitting up and looking at them.

This is just one example of how a rediscovered truth (see Matthew 10:7-8) has been preached by those who believe it and experienced by those who embrace it. To reject the practice of a now-revealed truth is to deny oneself the practical experience of that truth. Knowledge without the experience is fruitless.

I'll Take "the Works" on That

But someone will say, "You have faith, and I have works." Show me your faith without your works, and I will show you my faith BY MY WORKS.

James 2:18, Emphasis added

Believe Me that I am in the Father and the Father in Me, or else believe Me FOR THE SAKE OF THE WORKS THEMSELVES.

John 14:11, Emphasis added

Notice what follows closely on the heels of the preceding verse:

Most assuredly, I say to you, he who believes in Me, THE WORKS that I do he will do also; and GREATER WORKS than these he will do, because I go to My Father. And whatever you ask in My name, that I will do, that the Father may be glorified in the Son. If you ask anything in My name, I will do it."   John 14:12-14, Emphasis added

The criteria for *not* experiencing this truth are simple.

SUPERNATURAL

Don't believe it. Relegate it to the past. Disregard the idea that it has any relevance for you personally because:

- You haven't seen it.
- You haven't experienced it.
- You don't think you really need it.
- Your spiritual instructors say you can't have it.

Although it is changing, the majority of church faith in America is based on personal experience or the lack thereof. If a person hasn't had a certain experience, then they cannot seem to believe that it could be real. I've heard many people say, "If I see it, I'll believe it." But later, even after they *have* seen it, they still didn't believe it.

It isn't a sin to be unenlightened to specific truths of the Word of God, but once God shines His Light on a truth for a new generation and we reject it, then we are held accountable (see 1 Timothy 1:13 and James 4:17).

I would reiterate: I love being challenged in my thinking and my acting on the Word of God. I love experiencing the goodness and greatness of God. His mercy is everlasting, and I experientially relish that. I honor the men and women of God in the last five hundred years who have brought to the surface truths the Church had lost. Keep in mind that much of what you and I accept so naturally and unopposed today was formerly tested by strong opposition from within the church by those who were against any change in their tradition. It was the same in Jesus' day (see Mark 7:1-13), and it was the same in the time of the Great Reformation.

SHOW ME WHAT YOU'VE GOT

I wouldn't mind listening to a heresy hunter if only he had anything else to show me that works. But I'm not interested in dead works. If you're not seeing miracles, signs and wonders in your personal life and ministry, quite respectfully I doubt that you have anything I care to listen to. Jesus was confirmed by the Father through the miracles He did:

> *Men of Israel, hear these words: Jesus of Nazareth, a Man attested by God to you by miracles, wonders, and signs which God did through Him in your midst, as you yourselves also know.*
>
> Acts 2:22

This is the Man I want to follow, for we become like those we follow. How close on the heels of this Man are you? You can get even closer by following those who are ahead of you, men who are in hot pursuit of Him.

Don't reject a thought, a concept or a truth that your former instructor, mentor, pastor-teacher or spiritual father didn't preach—especially if they're already dead! They're not getting any new revelations. It is *"line upon line, precept upon precept, from glory to glory"* that we are to grow, and your spiritual fathers would surely not like to see you stagnated in your faith. It's not necessary to reject what they did or said, but if your growth in God is a closed box that can only contain what they did or said, you'll become a spiritual midget.

There are varying degrees of this concept. Perhaps one of the most extreme cases would be from the 1960s. William Branham was, to me, the most amazing prophet to emerge out of the great healing revival. I have read books about him, watched videos of his ministry and talked with those who attended his services. His was, without a doubt, an unprecedented gift that was in operation for modern times. His accuracy with words of knowledge and the prophetic was indeed a book-of-Acts operation.

Later, however, his unorthodox teachings and doctrines separated many from his ministry. After his untimely passing in 1965, a group of his followers began to gather together on Sundays and listen to tapes of his sermons. "What's wrong with that," some might ask? There's something wrong when a decade after a man dies we're still going to church on Sunday to listen to a cassette tape of something he preached many years before. Did God stop speaking when that one man died?

"SIR, WE WISH TO SEE JESUS"

God spoke to Moses face to face, and he, in turn, spoke to the people (see Exodus 33:11). Did God stop speaking to Israel when Moses died? Did He stop speaking because other Old Testament prophets died? Did He stop revealing Himself when Peter, Paul or John died? Did He stop speaking because John G. Lake, Smith Wigglesworth, A.A. Allen, John Wimber or Kenneth E. Hagin, Sr., died? The answer, of course, is no—in each case.

It isn't wrong to glean from these great generals of the faith, and it isn't wrong to listen, read or study after them. But something becomes amiss when those past revelations are the *only* revelations I am open to. God is still speaking today.

Are you currently hearing a voice that is carrying the sounds of eternity in it? There is a way to recognize the voice that will take you to the next level. It is a voice that will push you past any stagnant spiritual contentment you may currently have. It will cause your hunger for God to be enlarged. It will challenge your perspective on the kingdom you're building, yours or His. And, ultimately, it will always point you beyond a voice crying in the wilderness—to Jesus Himself:

> *Again, the next day, John stood with two of his disciples. And looking at Jesus as He walked, he said, "Behold the Lamb of God!" The two disciples heard him speak, and they followed Jesus.*
>
> John 1:35-37

A voice like this is one that is building God's Kingdom. Although John's voice was well known to the nation, it always pointed past the person speaking, to Jesus. This

111

SUPERNATURAL

will be true of every voice today that is advancing Heaven's agenda.

Warning: Roadblock Ahead!

Jesus also warned of a ministry to avoid. This is a voice you want to run from! The goal of the people of this ministry is to build their own kingdom. Their kingdoms may include (but are not necessarily limited to) personal ministry, pastoral ministry (a local church) or perhaps entire denominations or movements. Their concern is what makes them look good. At heart, they are driven by pride, control and manipulation. Jesus said of them:

> *But do not do according to their works; for they say, and do not do. For they bind heavy burdens, hard to bear, and lay them on men's shoulders; but they themselves will not move them with one of their fingers. But all their works they do to be seen by men.* Matthew 23:3-5

As a matter of fact, Jesus went on to say that not only are these men building their own kingdom; they are actually hindering others from building His true Kingdom:

> *But woe to you, scribes and Pharisees, hypocrites! For you shut up the kingdom of heaven against men; for you neither go in yourselves, nor do you allow those who are entering to go in.*
> Matthew 23:13

THE GOOD NEWS

Fortunately, there is a current stream flowing today that has allowed mixing of different denominations, non-denominations, backgrounds and cultures that is based on one thing and one thing only—Jesus and revival. It is built on relationships. The term you hear used most often is *apostolic networking*. This godly union of believers has allowed those who were former Baptists (myself included), Methodists, Lutherans, Church of God, Assembly of God and countless other forms of independent Charismatic groups to unite together in worship and demonstration of the Spirit. This move has allowed others to remain within their denomination without reprisal, while still being able to flow with what the Spirit is doing.

I believe a better understanding of what is being done would be the use of the word *alliance*. While everyone may not cross the same "t's" or dot the same "i's", we have allied ourselves together with one common goal—*"to destroy the works of the devil,"* whatever that takes! Our purpose is to bring the reality of an open heaven through miracles, healings, signs and wonders. Our fellowship is centered on God's Kingdom, and all that we do is for His glory.

"THROW THE BALL, I'M OPEN!"

A short time ago, I enjoyed lunch with Lamar Junkins,[3] a former Vineyard pastor from Birmingham, Alabama.

We had met previously at his church when he was hosting a conference featuring Bill Johnson. We basked together for over three hours, talking of nothing but Jesus and revival. Thank God for a patient waitress (whom we blessed, by the way). He talked of the loss of his spiritual father and how, for years, he had been looking for the one "who was carrying the ball now." This simple term meant who, at present, was carrying the impartation for revival.

Our discussion turned to Bill Johnson, the reason I had gone to Birmingham. In this man, we had found a voice that carried the weight of eternity. It wasn't that we were not hearing God's voice through others. We were. This, however, was the voice that was personally challenging us at that very moment in our pursuit of God's Kingdom.

There are many great ministries that are currently carrying the Word of the Lord, far too many to name. As Christ's Church, we owe it to a lost and dying world to demonstrate His love for His Kingdom now more than ever.

Who are you listening to? Where are you going? What are you going to do to establish His Kingdom in your world? Do you even know whose team you're on? It's time to get off the bench and back in the game. "Put me in, Coach. I'm tired of sitting out." It really isn't that difficult.

On God's team, everyone gets to play. Everyone gets

to carry the ball. Everyone gets to run. Everyone can go out for a pass. So, go long!

End Notes:

1. Alley, John Kingsley; *The Apostolic Revelation: The Reformation of the Church* Surprise, Arizona; (Selah Publishing Group: 2002)
2. Mel Bond is pastor of Agape Church in Wentzville, Missouri. He is an author and miracle revivalist doing crusades globally. www.agapechurch.addr.com
3. Lamar Junkins is pastor of the River Church of Birmingham, Alabama. www.riverchurchbirmingham.org

EPILOGUE

The book of Acts gives us insight into a transitional season for the early church from law to grace, from rules to relationship. It reveals an ongoing work of the Spirit of God intervening supernaturally in the lives of men and women. To be precise, it is the Acts of the Holy Spirit through the lives of ordinary humans, giving Him permission to advance the Kingdom through them.

Acts doesn't possess a concluding chapter, simply because the Holy Spirit didn't cease to *act* when the New Testament Scriptures were canonized for a new church age. Neither can we simply produce a concluding chapter today as if the supernatural realms of God were to cease.

The reality of this natural world will, without a doubt, succumb to the *real* world of the Kingdom of Heaven on earth. Regardless of eschatological positions on end-time events, as to when, where and how the King will reign, it is inevitable. His kingdom will come, and His reign will be forever and ever.

Until these events unfold, we will continue to live in the supernatural realm of God's favor upon His people, living and breathing the realities of Heaven's domain apprehending earth's possessions and bringing them under the control of the King of Kings.

A CHANGE IS GONNA COME!

Not unlike the days of John the Baptist, who heralded the day of the coming Messiah, Jesus, the anointed one, I believe we, too, are a type of forerunner who will bring transition. Just as John's arrival upset the ecclesiastical mode of the day, so also will this generation of supernatural sons and daughters bring division, as the new transition takes on reform.

Some will blindly continue their church in a box, even as a spiritual shift takes place around them from Church Age to Kingdom Age. They didn't see change coming in the time of John the Baptist, and neither will they see it coming in this day:

While Annas and Caiaphas were high priests, the word of God came to John the son of Zacharias in the wilderness. Luke 3:2

No, it was business as usual for religion: the greetings in the market place, the reserved seats in the synagogue, the recognition at the ministerial luncheons. Their job security was in tact. It was a good day to be a high priest. Meanwhile, back at the ranch ... a locust-eating prophet was preparing to emerge from the wilderness. What could possibly go wrong?

WHAT GOES AROUND ...

There seems to be a pattern throughout the Scriptures. Whenever things become comfortable in the spiritual arena, God comes along and shakes things up, often with controversial methods that require a choosing of sides.

When God moves, frequently it will be debated as to whether or not it really *is* God. Debate will swirl around things ranging from manifestations to messages, to the men or women God uses. This puts a lot of pressure on those to whom the people look for guidance and direction. Right or wrong, they have an office or a position to uphold. Times may change, but the circumstances do not.

Over and over again, when the time comes for a monumental shift spiritually, God looks for the most unlikely candidates to fulfill His purpose. He deliberately goes against religious standards of acceptance and chooses those with the least likely voice of authority (*exousia*), that He might add His power (*dunamis*) to it. His Word declares:

> **But God has chosen the foolish things of the world to put to shame the wise, and God has chosen the weak things of the world to put to shame the things which are mighty.** 1 Corinthians 1:27

God prophetically denounced the priesthood of Eli through the voice of a child. Moses, who complained of his weakness of speech, became the voice of judgment to an entire nation and the voice of deliverance to another. Gideon argued that his family was the weakest in Manasseh and that he was the least in his father's house. Still, using a minority, he overcame the majority.

THE LONGER THE PREPARATION
THE GREATER THE PURPOSE

Seemingly from out of nowhere, God will raise up a voice, to speak, demonstrate and reveal His purpose to a new generation. But what may appear to be an overnight sign and wonder usually is the culmination of years of preparation in God's secret service. Those who have endured the wilderness of adversity and the caves of obscurity are, more often than not, the same ones who will shake a nation for the glory of God.

It is in those lonely places that we learn to hear the voice of the Lord. The wilderness is a deserted place. It is a place of separation from the things of life, to the things of LIFE!

Don't expect to be bombarded with invitations to speak at the latest conference when you're in the wilderness. Don't anticipate your phone to ring off the hook with requests to speak at your best friend's church when you find yourself in the desert. Don't expect to be surrounded with the most popular and prosperous people of the day when your refuge is the cave of Adullam. Like David, you may be surrounded with those who are in distress, in debt and discontented (see 1 Samuel 22:1-2). David must have loved waking up every morning with that crowd!

It was in this type of setting that God chose to raise up a voice that would shake the nation:

As it is written in the book of the words of Isaiah the prophet, saying: "The voice of one crying in the wilderness: 'Prepare the way of the LORD; Make His paths straight.'" Luke 3:4

Verse 2 tells us, *"The word of God came to John the son of Zacharias in the wilderness."* It was in a desert place that

John attuned his ears and his heart to the voice of God. It is when we become isolated that the fine-tuning work of the Holy Spirit can be accomplished in us. It is when every other voice that has clamored for our attention has been silenced that the voice of the Lord comes through with the greatest clarity. It isn't that He hasn't been speaking, but, rather that we have been hard of hearing.

LED BY EXAMPLE

Don't automatically assume that the wilderness is from the enemy. On the contrary, it is God who will move us into seclusion to gain our attention, our trust and our faith. When we embrace the wilderness of isolation, it is then that God can entrust us with the power to accomplish His purpose. The hardest test for most of us is simply to recognize that it is the hand of God moving us toward our greatest destiny.

Are we greater than our Master? Will the Father expect less of us than of our Teacher and Example? Jesus Himself, although He was full of the Spirit, was *"led by the Spirit into the wilderness"* (Luke 4:1). After His wilderness experience, He returned *"in the power of the Spirit"* (Luke 4:14). It was only then, after His desert experience, that He began His earthly ministry.

Whether a test lasts forty days or forty years, only God knows the exact time required to prepare each of us for the power to accomplish His purpose. John's emergence from the wilderness wreaked havoc on the religious system of his day. The anointing of an Elijah shook a nation, created a political upheaval and prepared the way for the Messiah.

In the end, it cost John his head. There is always a price to be paid for the anointing. For most of us, it is called "enduring the preparation."

BLOW THE TRUMPET IN ZION

Somewhere some "Annases" and "Caiaphases" are alive and well today, comfortable and content, wrapped securely in their sacred robes of religion. They have no fear and no worry. No one's rocking their boat. Their calendar is packed. The press is happy. The pews are occupied. And the coffers are full.

But somewhere there's a wilderness turning into an oasis. Somewhere there's a cave emptying its occupants for war. There is a new "Desert Storm" on the horizon.

What could possibly go wrong?

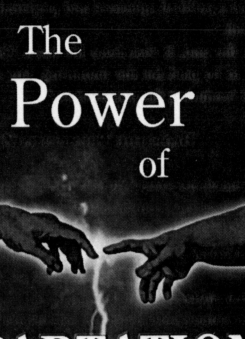

The
Power
of

IMPARTATION

THE NEED FOR
DIVINE APPOINTMENTS
WITH SPIRITUAL FATHERS

Eddie T. Rogers

MINISTRY CONTACT INFORMATION

Revival in Power
Eddie and Michelle Rogers

Visit us on the World Wide Web for contact information, updates, new products, and devotionals at:

www.revivalinpower.com

— Notes —

Printed in the United States
200007BV00002B/118-222/A